simple
pleasures

simple
pleasures

incredibly craveable recipes for everyday cooking

jodi moreno

photography by david alvarado

Gibbs Smith

CONTENTS

Introduction

My grandparents on my mother's side were immigrants from Italy, which meant I grew up with things like pasta drying on the washing machine, family dinners with that same pasta on Sunday afternoons, dollops of homemade ricotta on top of that pasta, vegetables picked from the garden at every meal, pancakes on Tuesdays, Bolognese on birthdays, and the smell of cooked tomatoes forever filling the entire home. Food was everything, and every meal was something to be carefully considered and celebrated.

I have always recognized how lucky I am to have grown up with a ritual of home-cooked meals. Both my grandmother and my mother's home cooking have had a huge influence on my love affair with the everyday pleasures of delicious food. When I was young, I thought that all grandmothers had a garden in their backyard and they cooked for their families for every meal. It wasn't until I left home and lived on my own that I realized how lucky I was to grow up with all that incredible home cooking and connected family time around the table.

My life and relationship with food since then has taken a long and winding but delicious road. My passion for food, my curiosity around different cultures, and my obsession with traveling, tasting, exploring, and discovering is at the heart of everything I do.

All of this eventually led me to choose a path as a chef, where food would be the soul of my everyday life. Little did I know that this path would also lead me to one day completely uproot my entire life in New York to follow my tastes, senses, and desires to another country that loves to celebrate food as much as I do. A place that I became fascinated with and fell madly and deeply in love with, enough to make it my new home.

I now find myself just like my grandparents, as an immigrant to another country. With my move to Mexico a few years ago, I found myself wanting to relive my most nostalgic food memories as a way to experience some of my favorite comfort foods from home. At the same time, I was trying to learn as much as I could while living in one of the most interesting and exciting countries for food in the world. Moving to a different country truly gave me a new and fresh perspective on cooking, and being around all of these incredible ingredients was intoxicating. During those early days, I challenged myself to experiment with those ingredients as a way to learn new recipes and techniques. It has been incredibly eye-opening, and I am now so grateful for the way this time has shaped, pushed, and enhanced my cooking and tastes in so many ways.

With the restrictions placed on us during the pandemic, normal routines and social activities were canceled, and like many of us, I was forced to rediscover the things that I loved to do at home. For the first time in ages, I was truly cooking and creating with my heart. I was alone, so there was no one to feed, no one to impress, and no one's tastes to consider but my own. I was able to learn what truly nourished me. As it turns out, I am

drawn to so many of the recipes I grew up with. I craved the familiar pastas that reminded me of my grandmother, the comforting desserts my mom used to make, along with all of the simplest pleasures like bread, butter, juicy tomatoes, and perfect avocados. I used to think that food had to be 100 percent healthy to be nurturing, but during this sweet time I found that comforting food can be the ultimate form of nourishment.

The most important thing I learned during this time is that slowing down and enjoying life's simple pleasures is something to be celebrated—and always should be. My family recipes and food memories became more important to me than ever before. Little comforts made the days feel lighter, and familiar tastes became such an important part of my day to day.

I spend as much time dining out as I do cooking at home, for friends, or for work, and if there is one thing I have learned, it's that people love the familiar. For me, that familiarity is one of the true simple pleasures in life. And that is what this book is all about—recipes for the best, most familiar, most pleasurable meals, done in the simplest way possible.

There is such elegance in simplicity. I feel this so deeply, on every level. The perfect pasta with a simple red sauce, the freshest corn tortilla straight off the comal, warm crusty sourdough dipped in really good extra-virgin olive oil and sprinkled with crunchy sea salt, your favorite pair of jeans and broken-in T-shirt, sitting on your couch with the window open and a warm breeze, reading a book by candlelight at night. These really, truly are the best things in life.

Hopefully this book will help you tap into this simplicity and be a playful guide to enjoying life's simple pleasures each and every day.

GOOD MORNINGS

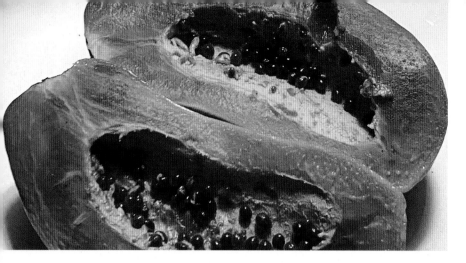

INTRO

the silence of an early morning.
a thick slice of pancakes.
the smell of dark roasted coffee.
the sound of sizzling bacon.
a runny egg yolk.
butter spread thick on toast.

While I love early mornings, I am not the biggest breakfast person. When I do make breakfast, I like to make it as tasty, creative, and simple as possible. My favorite thing about breakfast might be that these meals set the tone for the entire day.

Salsa Macha Fried Egg Taco with Sliced Avocado + Chives

SERVES 1

½ avocado, sliced

½ a lime, juiced

Kosher salt

1 tortilla

2 to 3 tablespoons Salsa Macha (page 194)

1 large egg

1 teaspoon chives, minced

This is probably my most-made, most-loved breakfast. It's quick and easy, satisfying, spicy, and most of all—delicious. Living in Mexico, I usually have things like fresh tortillas and salsa macha on hand, but this is also quite versatile if you don't have those specific ingredients around. You could swap a chili crisp (which is what this recipe is originally inspired by) or another salsa. Even leftover tomato sauce would work. You could also serve this on toasted bread instead of a tortilla. The additions and toppings are also endless, so you can really get wild and creative with this one.

PLACE the sliced avocado on a fresh tortilla. Add a squeeze of lime juice and season with salt.

HEAT a small frying pan (preferably nonstick) over medium heat. Add 2 to 3 tablespoons of salsa to the pan. When you start to see little bubbles, crack the egg into the center of the salsa. Allow the egg to cook for about 2 minutes while you gently spoon some of the salsa over the white parts of the egg to help cook and crisp up the edges a bit. Fry the egg to your desired temperature. (I like a sunny-side-up egg where the whites are cooked and the yolk is runny.)

SLIDE the egg and salsa out of the pan onto the tortilla with the avocado. Top with the chives and any other toppings you desire and enjoy immediately.

Grandpa's Pancakes with Maple Butter

My grandpa loved pancakes more than anyone I have ever met. When I was lucky enough to stay the night at my grandparents' house, he would tell me to ask my grandmother to make him a "thousand" of his favorite pancakes for breakfast. It was our little joke, and when I would then go to my grandmother and tell her that Poppy wanted a thousand pancakes, she would smile knowingly and roll her eyes. She then would heat up her cast-iron griddle and make my poppy's pancakes, stacked high on the plate, making them feel like a thousand paper-thin pancakes. This recipe is one of my favorite memories of my grandparents, and I think of them every time I make these pancakes. I know they would love my addition of compound maple butter as the perfect salty-sweet topping.

TO WHIP THE MAPLE BUTTER, place the softened butter, maple syrup, and cinnamon in a medium bowl and whisk until fully combined. You could also do this in a food processor if you prefer. This will make more butter than you will need for this pancake recipe, but you can roll it into a log, wrap it, and keep it in the fridge and use over a few months.

IN A MIXING BOWL, lightly beat the eggs, then add in the milk, maple syrup, and vanilla. Whisk to combine, then add the flour, baking powder, and salt. Whisk until fully combined; the batter should be quite runny.

HEAT 1 tablespoon butter and 1 tablespoon olive oil in a large frying pan over medium heat. Ladle about 1/3 cup of the batter for 1 pancake into the pan and cook until you start to see bubbles around the edges and coming up in the center of the pancake. That means it's ready to flip. Then cook for about 2 minutes on the other side until golden brown. Transfer to a plate or baking sheet and repeat until all of the batter has been cooked, adding more butter and olive oil as needed if the pan gets too dry.

I LOVE TO SERVE these pancakes in a big stack with a bit of the maple butter melted on top.

MAKES ABOUT 12 THIN PANCAKES

FOR THE MAPLE BUTTER

½ cup (1 stick) salted butter, softened

3 tablespoons pure maple syrup

Pinch of cinnamon

FOR THE PANCAKES

2 large eggs

1 cup whole milk

1 tablespoon pure maple syrup

1 teaspoon vanilla extract

1 cup all-purpose flour

1 teaspoon baking powder

Pinch of kosher salt

2 to 3 tablespoons unsalted butter, for cooking the pancakes

2 to 3 tablespoons extra-virgin olive oil, for cooking the pancakes

Giant Hash Brown with Crème Fraîche + Tomato Confit + Smoked Salmon

SERVES 1 TO 2

FOR THE HASH BROWN

1 large Idaho potato, peeled

Kosher salt, to taste

Freshly ground black pepper, to taste

1 scallion, thinly sliced; white and green parts separated

1 tablespoon unsalted butter

1 tablespoon extra-virgin olive oil

TOPPINGS + ADDITIONS

1 tablespoon crème fraîche, plain yogurt, or sour cream

¼ cup tomato confit (see How to Confit Any Vegetable, page 197) or 1 tomato, sliced

2 to 3 slices smoked salmon

Potatoes are one of my true loves, and I often find myself craving them in the morning. One morning, that craving hit and I happened to have one Idaho potato sitting around. I quickly peeled and shredded it, and within minutes of crisping it in the pan that craving was satisfied and a new simple, comforting breakfast was discovered. You can use this giant hash brown as a vehicle for whatever toppings you have on hand. I particularly love this version because it gives me a lox-and-bagel vibe, but I have also been known to top it with sautéed tomato and onion with bacon or even a massaged kale salad with a sunny-side-up egg.

USING A BOX GRATER, grate the potato into a medium bowl. Add the white part of the scallion (reserving the green for topping), season with salt and pepper, and allow it to sit for about 2 minutes. Then squeeze the grated potato mixture to release as much moisture as possible.

HEAT the butter and olive oil in a small frying pan over medium heat. Form the grated potato into a ball, then add it to the pan. Using the back of a spatula, flatten and form the hash brown by pushing on the sides to make a round shape that is about ½-inch thick. Cook for 3 to 5 minutes on each side until golden brown. Remove and transfer to a serving plate.

TOP with crème fraîche, tomato confit or tomato slices, smoked salmon, and remaining green scallion slices. Enjoy immediately.

Sesame-Crusted Brown-Butter Banana Bread with Honey + Crème Fraîche

A well-made classic banana bread is one of life's great sweet carb indulgences. I have been working on this version for years, making tiny tweaks and improvements and adding in a few improvements, such as the slightly nutty browned butter and a layer of sesame seeds and sugar on top for a sweet, crunchy texture. But the real magic happens if you go the extra step to fry the banana bread in butter and serve it with some crème fraîche, honey, and sea salt. I really cannot think of a better balance of all things sweet, tangy, crunchy, and salty to start the day (or for a pick-me-up anytime).

PREHEAT the oven to 350°F. Grease a 9 x 5-inch loaf pan with butter.

IN A LARGE MIXING BOWL, stir together the flour, sugar, baking soda, and salt.

HEAT a pan over medium heat, and add the butter. Melt the butter until it starts to bubble, then keep an eye on it, swirling it every so often until it starts to turn golden brown, about 3 to 4 minutes. Add the mashed banana to the pan and stir to combine it with the butter. Cook for another minute or so, then pour the brown butter–banana mixture into the mixing bowl with the dry ingredients and stir to incorporate.

ADD the egg and vanilla to the batter and stir to combine. Pour the batter into the greased loaf pan. Sprinkle 1 teaspoon sugar and a layer of sesame seeds on top. Bake for 50 minutes to 1 hour, until a cake tester comes out clean when inserted into the center. Let the bread cool in the pan for 5 to 10 minutes before removing and placing on a wire rack to cool completely, or you can leave it in the pan.

HEAT 1 to 2 tablespoons butter in a small frying pan. Add a slice of the banana bread and toast for 2 to 3 minutes on each side until slightly golden. Transfer to a plate and serve with a dollop of crème fraîche on the side, a drizzle of honey over top, and a sprinkle of sea salt.

MAKES 1 LOAF

1 cup all-purpose flour

1/2 cup granulated sugar, plus 1 teaspoon for topping

1 teaspoon baking soda

1/4 teaspoon kosher salt

1/2 cup (1 stick) unsalted butter, plus more for greasing

2 to 3 very ripe bananas, mashed (1 1/2 cups)

1 large egg, lightly beaten

2 teaspoons vanilla extract

3 to 4 tablespoons sesame seeds

TOPPINGS + ADDITIONS

1 to 2 tablespoons unsalted butter

1 tablespoon crème fraîche

Honey

Flaky sea salt

The Ultimate Breakfast Salad with Butter Lettuce + Soft-Boiled Egg

SERVES 1 TO 2

TOPPINGS + ADDITIONS

Sliced avocado

Sautéed mushrooms or any seasonal sautéed vegetable

Cooked quinoa

Nuts and seeds (such as almonds, pumpkin seeds, or sesame seeds), lightly toasted

Thinly sliced scallion or chives

Chopped fresh herbs, such as basil, mint, cilantro, or flat-leaf parsley

As often as I crave indulgent breakfasts, I also crave light and fresh things like salads in the mornings. I used to have a smoothie almost every morning for breakfast, but over time I got tired of "drinking" my breakfast. I still wanted something light and fresh, so I started replacing my smoothie with a refreshing breakfast salad that featured a bright, tart dressing laced with apple cider vinegar (another great way to start the day). I also like to add some protein to the salad—the best way in this salad is with a quick and easy soft-boiled egg, so you can get some of the yummy runny yolk coating the lettuce leaves.

This salad is a great canvas for whatever is in season in addition to whatever leftovers you might have that day. I love to add quickly sautéed mushrooms in the winter, asparagus in the spring, and leftover roasted squash in the fall. I always include an avocado, regardless of the season, and additionally some sesame seeds or pumpkin seeds for crunch. This is more of an inspirational nudge, rather than a formal recipe, to remind you that salad for breakfast is a good idea.

LETTUCE: I love butter lettuce for breakfast because it has a great texture and watery crunch. Any lettuce will do—I also love arugula or, in the winter, a bitter chicory.

DRESSING: I don't usually measure the dressing for my breakfast salad. It is usually a drizzle of this, a splash of that, or something that I already have that is homemade. Olive oil, apple cider vinegar, a pinch of salt, and some black pepper. Sometimes I use sesame oil and rice vinegar if I want more of those kinds of flavors.

SOFT-BOILED EGG: Prepare an ice bath, and bring a small pot of water to a boil. Drop the egg into the boiling water and then lower the heat to medium low. Cook for 6 minutes (for a runnier yolk) or up to 8 minutes (for a jammier yolk). Remove with a slotted spoon and transfer to the ice bath to stop the cooking. Peel, slice in half, and serve over the salad.

Caramelized Bananas over Buttery Oats

SERVES 1

FOR THE OATS

2 tablespoons unsalted butter, divided

1 cup rolled oats

1 cup milk, regular or plant-based

Pinch of kosher salt

FOR THE BANANA

1 tablespoon unsalted butter

1 tablespoon extra-virgin olive oil

1 banana, sliced lengthwise or cut into cubes

TOPPINGS + ADDITIONS

Sprinkle of cinnamon

Nuts and seeds, such as toasted almond or pistachios

Blueberries, raspberries, or strawberries (roasted in a pan so they become a little saucy)

Shredded coconut flakes (unsweetened)

Drizzle of honey or pure maple syrup

Butter

I started making this delicious dish for my mom when I was taking care of her when she was sick. One of my mom's favorite desserts was bananas Foster, so one morning when I was making breakfast for her and wanted to cheer her up, I had the idea to caramelize some bananas in a pan and serve them over oats. It quickly became one of her favorites, and mine too. I crave this sweet dish regularly and love to mix it up with all sorts of other toppings and variations.

MELT 1 tablespoon butter in a small saucepan and add the oats. Toast for 1 minute, then add the milk and salt. Cook for 2 to 3 minutes, until the milk has almost been absorbed completely by the oats. Turn off the heat, add the remaining 1 tablespoon, and let it sit while you prepare the bananas.

IN A SMALL FRYING PAN, heat the butter and olive oil over medium heat. Add the banana and cook for 2 to 3 minutes on each side until golden brown and caramelized. You will want to use a spatula to flip because sometimes the sugars from the banana will cause it to stick to the pan.

TRANSFER the oatmeal to a plate or bowl and top with the banana and any other desired toppings.

Ginger-Scallion Egg Drop Breakfast Broth

One of the most comforting and nourishing breakfasts I like to indulge in is to take bone broth and add an egg to it, along with other flavors and healthy aromatics like ginger and scallion. It's basically like a more classically known egg drop soup but for breakfast. Years ago, I jumped on the trend of having bone broth in the morning instead of coffee because of its many health benefits, and it has stuck with me and is something I often have when I need a little immune boost in the morning. The egg adds protein, so it's more filling than the broth alone, and it also gives the soup a breakfast vibe. It's most important to use either homemade broth or a very high-quality store-bought broth. Some other great additions include freshly ground turmeric, a handful of chopped leafy greens such as spinach or kale, or a cup of any kind of cooked, chopped vegetable such as carrot or zucchini.

COMBINE the broth, garlic, and ginger in a saucepan and bring to a boil. Lower the heat and, while stirring, add in the beaten egg. Cook for about 2 minutes, continuously stirring, until the egg is cooked. Remove from the heat, add the scallions and any other toppings you like, and serve.

SERVES 1

2 cups homemade or high-quality store-bought bone broth

1 garlic clove, pressed

1 (1-inch) piece of fresh ginger, peeled and grated

1 egg, lightly beaten

2 scallions, green parts only, thinly sliced

Everything Breakfast Biscuit Sandwich with Bacon, Cheese + Chive Butter

MAKES 8 BISCUITS

FOR THE BISCUITS

2$\frac{1}{2}$ cups all-purpose flour

1 tablespoon baking powder (aluminum-free)

1 teaspoon kosher salt

8 tablespoons ($\frac{1}{2}$ cup) very cold, unsalted butter, cubed

1 cup buttermilk

Everything Seasoning (see below)

FOR THE EVERYTHING SEASONING

2 tablespoons poppy seeds

1 tablespoon white sesame seeds

1 tablespoon black sesame seeds

1 tablespoon dried minced garlic

1 tablespoon dried minced onion

2 teaspoons flaky sea salt

FOR THE CHIVE BUTTER

8 tablespoons (1 stick) salted butter, softened

$\frac{1}{4}$ to $\frac{1}{2}$ cup chives, minced

TOPPINGS + ADDITIONS

Fried eggs

Bacon or ham, cooked

Cheese (Asiago, cheddar, or Gruyère), sliced

I believe a homemade breakfast sandwich should be an important part of your breakfast arsenal. Especially for weekends when there is time and energy to make something fun and a bit indulgent. Egg and cheese are must; bacon or another breakfast meat are optional but encouraged. You can really take it to another level by making your own buttery biscuit to serve it on. Biscuits are an easy entry into breadmaking. Even better, you can make and store the dough in your freezer so when a biscuit breakfast sandwich craving hits, all you need to do is give the biscuits a quick toss into the oven.

PREHEAT the oven to 425°F.

PREPARE the everything seasoning: Combine all ingredients in a small bowl and mix well. This should make about $\frac{1}{2}$ cup of seasoning—slightly more than you'll need for these 8 biscuits.

FOR THE BISCUITS, place the flour, baking powder, and salt into a large bowl. Using your fingers, press the butter chunks into the flour until you have little clumps.

MAKE a well in the center of the butter-flour mixture and add the buttermilk. Mix everything together and form it into a ball, being mindful not to overwork the dough. It should be a little shaggy and crumbly. Then transfer the dough to a floured work surface. Using floured hands, press the dough into a rectangle that is roughly 1-inch thick. Fold one side of the rectangle into the center and the other on top. Turn the dough horizontally and repeat the process of flattening it into a 1-inch thick rectangle and folding in the sides. Do this three times, ending with it in the rectangle shape.

USING A BISCUIT CUTTER OR A GLASS, cut the biscuits into rounds. I prefer to cook these in a large cast-iron skillet, but they can also be baked on a parchment-lined baking sheet. Arrange the biscuits in the cast-iron skillet or baking sheet, close together. Sprinkle the top with the everything seasoning. Bake for approximately 20 minutes, until the tops are golden brown.

WHILE THE BISCUITS ARE BAKING, make the chive butter. Combine the softened butter and chives in a bowl. There will be extra; it will keep in the fridge for 4 to 6 weeks.

TO ASSEMBLE THE SANDWICH, spread the chive butter onto the biscuit, then top with the egg, bacon or ham, and cheese of your choice.

Leftover Fried Rice Bowl with Avocado + Sesame + Herbs

I love to have cooked rice in the fridge for when I want to make something quick and easy. Sometimes that rice is left over from something I made the night before or from a takeout order when I make sure to get extra white rice on the side. Often, the quick and easy meal I make with that leftover rice ends up being for breakfast—and in this case, a breakfast version of fried rice.

My breakfast fried rice has egg and veggies, and it can also have some other kind of protein if that is the mood. I adjust the flavors to whatever I feel like in the early morning, which is usually a little lighter than a more traditional fried rice you would find in a restaurant. This means that I generally include lots of fresh herbs or greens, and avocado is a must to round out the flavors.

MELT the butter in a large skillet over medium heat. Add the spinach and cook for 1 to 2 minutes until wilted. Add the eggs and cook while stirring to break up the eggs a bit. Once the eggs are cooked a bit, about 1 minute, add the rice and stir to combine and continue to break up the egg. Add the scallions, soy sauce, and sesame oil and cook for another minute. Taste and adjust the seasoning to taste.

TRANSFER to a plate and top with sliced avocado, a sprinkle of the sesame seeds, a handful of herbs, and some salsa macha or chili crisp.

SERVES 2

1 to 2 tablespoons unsalted butter

1 cup spinach or another leafy green, loosely packed and finely chopped

2 eggs, lightly beaten

Approximately 1 cup leftover white rice

2 scallions, thinly sliced

1 teaspoon soy sauce or tamari

$\frac{1}{2}$ teaspoon sesame oil

TOPPINGS + ADDITIONS

$\frac{1}{2}$ an avocado, sliced

1 teaspoon sesame seeds

Fresh herbs, such as cilantro, basil, mint, or flat-leaf parsley

Chili crisp or Salsa Macha (page 194) (optional)

SALAD DAYS

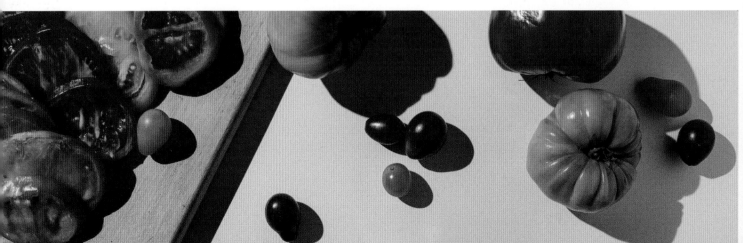

INTRO

crisp, cold romaine on a hot summer day.
a perfectly ripe heirloom tomato.
pink bitter chicory to brighten up a cold day.
salads as the main event.
the beauty of a simple vinaigrette.

A well-made, perfectly balanced salad is one of life's little joys. Whether it is meant to be an accompaniment to other dishes or the main event, a beautiful salad is always a welcome addition to any table. Salads are the perfect canvas for exploring flavors and textures and discovering how they can enhance each other.

Celery Caesar Salad
with Bacon Breadcrumbs

SERVES 4

**FOR THE BACON
BREADCRUMBS**

3 slices bacon

½ cup panko breadcrumbs

Kosher salt

Freshly ground black pepper

FOR THE DRESSING

3 oil-packed anchovy filets

1 large garlic clove

Kosher salt

Freshly ground black pepper

1 large egg yolk, room temperature

2 tablespoons fresh lemon juice

½ teaspoon Dijon mustard

⅔ cup vegetable oil

¼ cup grated Parmesan cheese, plus some
more for topping the salad

FOR THE SALAD

3 celery stalks, halved and julienned

3 romaine hearts, trimmed and torn in half
or quarters

When it comes to things as iconic as a Caesar salad, I typically like to keep it classic and work toward perfecting the technique. But that was before I was inspired to try some crisp, thinly sliced celery and smoky bacon–laced breadcrumbs to enhance the already perfect balance in a Caesar salad. And it truly does. There is something about that extra-fresh crunch from the celery and the way that the breadcrumbs coat the leaves and dressing (in lieu of the cumbersome crouton) that really takes a classic Caesar to another level.

TO MAKE THE BREADCRUMBS, cook the bacon in a frying pan over medium heat until it is well done and crisp, and transfer it to a paper towel–lined plate to remove excess oil. Then transfer the bacon to a food processor and pulse until you have a fine crumb. Add the panko to the food processor and pulse just a couple of times to incorporate. Taste and add a pinch or two of salt and black pepper, as you feel it is necessary. Set aside until you're ready to assemble the salad.

TO MAKE THE DRESSING, place the anchovies and garlic onto a cutting board with a pinch of salt and some ground black pepper and mince together until the mixture forms a smooth paste. Transfer to a bowl with the egg yolk, lemon juice, and mustard and whisk to combine. Then add the oil in a slow stream while whisking until the dressing is a thick, creamy consistency. Add in the grated Parmesan, and taste and adjust the seasoning if necessary.

TO ASSEMBLE THE SALAD, place the lettuce and celery in a large serving bowl. Add the dressing while tossing to evenly coat the leaves until they are sufficiently dressed. Finish with the breadcrumbs and some additional Parmesan and black pepper. Serve immediately.

Tomato Burrata Salad (Tomatoes Three Ways!)

Salads are all about the freshness of the ingredients. This guiding principle is never truer than it is for a tomato salad. Each of these three different preparations highlights the best of each type of tomato, so choosing the juiciest, ripest tomatoes and using the freshest burrata and high-quality olive oil is crucial. You could use mozzarella instead of burrata, but the burrata gives it a beautiful creamy texture. This salad also calls for some crusty bread to be served on the side to soak up the extra sauce made from the tomatoes and burrata.

PREHEAT the oven to 400°F. Place the cherry tomatoes on a parchment-lined baking sheet. Drizzle with olive oil and season with salt and black pepper. Roast the tomatoes for 20 to 30 minutes, until the tomatoes are very tender. Remove, and allow to cool to room temperature.

USING A GRATER, grate the plum tomatoes into a bowl, discarding the skins. Press or grate (using a microplane) the garlic clove into the tomato puree. Season with salt and pepper and add a generous drizzle of olive oil.

USING A MEDIUM-SIZED SERVING PLATE, spread the grated plum tomatoes onto the bottom of the plate. Layer the sliced heirloom tomatoes on top, and season them with salt and pepper. Then tear the burrata and spread it evenly over the top of the tomatoes and season with salt and black pepper and drizzle with olive oil. Lastly, place the roasted cherry tomatoes on top and distribute the basil leaves evenly. Serve with a baguette or toasted bread on the side.

SERVES 4 TO 6

12 cherry (or small variety) tomatoes

Extra-virgin olive oil

Kosher salt

Freshly ground black pepper

2 very ripe, plum tomatoes

1 garlic clove

1 large (or 2 medium) ripe heirloom tomatoes, thinly sliced

4 to 8 ounces burrata cheese (or mozzarella cheese)

10 to 12 fresh basil leaves

A baguette on the side, for serving

Pickle Potato Salad
with Crispy Mortadella

SERVES 2 TO 4

1 pound baby potatoes (red, yellow, or a mix)

Kosher salt

FOR THE SAUCE

²⁄₃ cup mayonnaise

2 tablespoons Dijon mustard

1 tablespoon pickle juice (either a dill pickle or a jalapeño if you want some spice)

¹⁄₂ teaspoon kosher salt

Freshly ground black pepper

TOPPINGS + ADDITIONS

4 ounces mortadella, thinly sliced into strips

Extra-virgin olive oil

2 scallions, thinly sliced

¹⁄₂ cup diced yellow peperoncini or guindillas

For me, a classic potato salad falls into the category of essential recipes to have in your go-to repertoire. When made right, it has the potential to be the star of your summertime feasts. I remember the first time I brought potato salad to a beach barbecue, and I made a version where I blended some crispy bacon into the sauce. Needless to say, those bacon-laced potatoes were a massive hit. Later, I became obsessed with the magic of pickle brine—especially adding it to sauces or dressings, and obviously potato salad felt like the perfect match. Here I am switching out bacon for crispy mortadella, which feels like a very appropriate update. With those two twists combined, a next-level, go-to potato salad was born.

PLACE the potatoes in a large pot and add water to cover by about 2 inches. Add 1 table-spoon salt to the water, bring the water to a boil, and cook the potatoes until just fork tender, about 10 to 15 minutes from once it starts boiling. Drain the potatoes, transfer to a serving bowl, and allow to cool.

WHILE THE POTATOES ARE COOKING, prepare the sauce. Whisk together the mayonnaise, mustard, and pickle juice in a small mixing bowl. Season with ¹⁄₂ teaspoon salt and some freshly ground black pepper. Taste and adjust the seasoning as necessary.

HEAT a drizzle of olive oil in a medium-sized skillet over medium heat. Sauté the morta-della until crispy, about 1 to 2 minutes on each side. Remove from heat and set aside until you're ready to assemble and serve.

ONCE THE POTATOES ARE COOL ENOUGH to touch, lightly smash them by using the palm of your hand. Pour the sauce over the potatoes and toss to combine. Sprinkle the scallions and peperoncini on top and toss again. Top with the crispy mortadella and serve.

Sesame Crunch Chicken Salad with Marinated Cucumbers

This super-refreshing, satisfying salad has so many layers of flavor and texture. By individually dressing each tier of the salad and layering them in a specific order, each bite is bursting with unique flavors. While the layering is super important, you can stray from the recipe by swapping out or adding certain ingredients. If there is another veggie you want to add to the salad, julienne it and throw in it with the cabbage. And if you want to substitute tahini (for an extra sesame kick) or plain whole-milk Greek yogurt for the mayonnaise in the dressing, that would be great as well—just make sure if you're using tahini to thin it out with about $1/3$ cup water before mixing with the other ingredients.

IN A SMALL BOWL, toss the cucumbers with the oil, vinegar, and a pinch of salt and let them marinate for approximately 15 minutes while you make the rest of the salad.

TO MAKE THE DRESSING, place all the ingredients into a small bowl and whisk to combine.

ROUGHLY CHOP the shredded chicken. Transfer to a large serving bowl along with cabbage, scallions, radishes, jalapeño, and 1 tablespoon neutral oil. Season to taste with salt and black pepper. Pour the dressing over the chicken and vegetables and toss to combine.

TOP with the marinated cucumbers, mint, basil, and a heavy sprinkle of the sesame seeds. Serve immediately.

SERVES 4

FOR THE CUCUMBERS

1 to 2 baby cucumbers, thinly sliced (about 1 cup)

1 tablespoon neutral vegetable oil , such as grapeseed or sunflower

1 tablespoon seasoned rice wine vinegar

$1/2$ teaspoon kosher salt

FOR THE DRESSING

$1/3$ cup mayonnaise

1 tablespoon seasoned rice wine vinegar

1 teaspoon soy sauce or tamari

1 teaspoon sesame oil

FOR THE SALAD

$1/2$ roasted chicken, meat pulled from bones and shredded (about 2 cups)

$1/2$ head green cabbage (about 4 cups)

3 scallions, thinly sliced

2 radishes, thinly sliced

1 jalapeño, seeded and finely chopped

1 tablespoon neutral oil

Kosher salt

Freshly ground black pepper

TOPPINGS + ADDITIONS

10 fresh mint leaves, thinly sliced

10 fresh basil leaves, thinly sliced

2 tablespoons toasted sesame seeds

Endive Salad with Honey, Cream + Crispy Coppa

SERVES 4

FOR THE COPPA

3 to 4 ounces coppa or other cured sausage, sliced

Extra-virgin olive oil

FOR THE HONEY CREAM

½ cup heavy cream, crème fraîche, or plain whole-milk Greek yogurt

1 small garlic clove, pressed

1 tablespoon fresh lemon juice

¼ teaspoon kosher salt

Freshly ground black pepper

2 teaspoons of honey

FOR THE SALAD

3 whole endives, leaves separated

Drizzle of extra-virgin olive oil

Kosher salt

Freshly ground black pepper

This salad is perfect example of the ultimate balance between bitter, sweet, salty, savory, creamy, and tangy. I also love that this is done in such a simple way, making this salad equally impressive in taste as it is in ease. The recipe calls for heavy cream but you can substitute a plain Greek yogurt for a slightly lighter version. Also, feel free to switch the coppa (an Italian cured sausage) with another type of cured meat, such as prosciutto or pepperoni.

For this salad I prefer to serve the dressing on the bottom and then dredge the endive and coppa when eating, but you can also toss the endive with the dressing as well.

HEAT the olive oil in a medium skillet over medium heat. Add the coppa and cook for about 2 minutes on each side until crisp. Set aside.

IN A SMALL BOWL, whisk together the cream or yogurt with the garlic, lemon juice, salt, and black pepper. Then pour the dressing in the bottom of a bowl or plate. Drizzle the honey over the top of the dressing.

PLACE the endive leaves on top of the creamy dressing. Add the crisped coppa on top, distributing evenly. Finish with a drizzle of olive oil, a sprinkle of salt, and some freshly cracked pepper. Enjoy immediately.

Arugula Herb Salad
with Lemon + Parmesan

SERVES 4 TO 6

2 handfuls arugula (about 4 cups)

Drizzle of good-quality extra-virgin olive oil

Juice from ½ lemon

Approximately 12 fresh basil leaves, torn

¼ cup flat-leaf parsley leaves, loosely packed

Pinch of kosher salt

Freshly ground black pepper

¼ to ½ cup shaved Parmesan cheese

You might think that this salad doesn't need an official recipe, but it was something I had to include because it is one that I serve so often beside a favorite pasta. I am even known to throw it shamelessly right on top of the pasta itself as the ultimate finishing touch.

This salad can be made in minutes, and it is especially perfect for when you might want something green and light alongside something more indulgent. It's another "non-recipe" where I don't really measure—I just add a drizzle of this and a pinch of that. This salad could be used as a base for some seasonal roasted vegetables— squash in the winter, tomatoes in the summer. It would also be great with a crunch element, such as a breadcrumbs, croutons, or toasted nuts and seeds.

PLACE the arugula onto a serving platter. Drizzle with the olive oil and lemon juice. Add the basil, parsley, salt, and black pepper and toss it all to combine. I like to use my hands to make sure all the leaves are evenly coated. Add the shaved Parmesan on top and serve immediately.

Layered Salad with Crème Fraîche + Pickle Ranch Dressing

This salad is one of my fondest food memories from when I was growing up. It was my mom's go-to recipe for summer barbecue parties. It is a quintessential '80s dish—the kind of easy-to-throw-together recipe with that fun wow factor. My mom was the queen of that vibe, and this was one of her prize recipes. The taste is so nostalgic that I can still remember the feeling of biting into this salad and tasting all the layers, especially the crunchy bacon against the crisp lettuce, and the creamy dressing.

This is the type of adaptable recipe where you can layer whatever you have on hand or is in season. So instead of a recipe, I will make some suggestions and you can use that as a springboard for your own layered salad creation.

My mom always served this with ranch dressing on the side, so guests could dress it how they like. A fun idea would be to serve this with a couple of different dressings on the side if you want to turn it into a layered salad party! Lastly, I recommend serving this in a large glass bowl so that you can see and enjoy all the layers of beautiful ingredients.

PLACE all the ingredients in a small mixing bowl and whisk to combine. Can be made a day or two in advance. Please see the following page for layered salad recipe combinations.

SERVES 6 TO 8

FOR THE CRÈME FRAÎCHE + PICKLE RANCH DRESSING

½ cup mayonnaise

¼ cup crème fraîche or buttermilk

1 tablespoon juice from any kind of pickle, preferably dill pickle or a jalapeño for spice

1 garlic clove, pressed

2 tablespoons fresh chives, minced

¼ teaspoon onion powder

¼ teaspoon garlic powder

½ teaspoon kosher salt

Freshly ground black pepper

Layered
Salad Ideas

suggest to layer the ingredients from the bottom to the top starting with the first listed ingredient. I also suggest doing at least 2 layers of each ingredient.

Romaine or iceberg lettuce
Tomato
Bacon
Scallion
Feta or blue cheese

Shaved brussels sprouts + kale
Roasted beets
Crispy prosciutto
Goat cheese

Roasted butternut squash
Arugula
Walnuts
Red onion
Manchego cheese

Asparagus
Snap peas or fava beans
Radish
Spring onion
Parmesan cheese

Grilled corn
Tomatoes
Pickled jalapeños
Chives
Breadcrumbs
Arugula
Basil

Radicchio Panzanella with Roasted Salmon + Fennel + Crushed Olive Dressing

I have a deep love for radicchio. It's vibrant pink color is especially dazzling when the bitter leaves are in their prime during the winter months. Because of its bitter flavor, I find it especially fun to pair with salty, sweet, and rich flavors. In this version, the saltiness from the olives and the richness from the salmon create a little symphony of flavors that also get soaked up by and enhanced by the sourdough croutons. The salmon can be optional, but it makes this more of a main meal than a side dish.

PREHEAT the oven to 300°F. Season the salmon with salt and pepper and drizzle with olive oil. Line a baking sheet with parchment paper and layer half of the lemons on the parchment paper. Lay the salmon skin-side down on top of the lemons and then cover with the remaining lemon slices.

ROAST the salmon for about 20 minutes, until it's cooked through but still quite tender. You should be able to flake it easily with a fork when it's done. Remove and allow to cool. (You can place it in the fridge while you prepare the rest if you prefer the salmon chilled.)

PLACE the torn pieces of bread onto a baking sheet and drizzle with olive oil and season with salt and pepper. Toast for 5 to 10 minutes, until golden brown.

TO MAKE THE DRESSING, combine the olive oil, vinegar, and garlic in a small bowl. On a cutting board, crush the olives with the back of a knife and add them to the dressing. Season with salt and pepper.

TO ASSEMBLE THE SALAD, place the radicchio, fennel, and croutons into a large serving bowl. Break apart the salmon with a fork so you get flaky pieces, leaving the skin behind, then add flaked salmon on top of the salad. Pour the dressing over the salad, toss to combine, and serve immediately.

SERVES 2 TO 4

FOR THE SALMON

2 (6- to 8-ounce) skin-on salmon filets

Kosher salt

Freshly ground black pepper

Drizzle of olive oil

1 lemon, sliced

FOR THE CROUTONS

Approximately 2 cups torn sourdough bread or baguette (about 1 to 1½-inch pieces)

Drizzle of olive oil

Kosher salt

Freshly ground black pepper

FOR THE CRUSHED OLIVE DRESSING

¼ cup extra-virgin olive oil

2 teaspoons white wine vinegar

1 garlic clove, grated or pressed

1 cup olives, preferably Castelvetrano

Kosher salt

Freshly ground black pepper

FOR THE SALAD

2 heads radicchio, leaves separated

1 fennel bulb, thinly shaved on a mandolin

Tomatoes + Cucumber + Banana Peppers over Whipped Feta

SERVES 2

Whipped Feta (page 83)

2 heirloom tomatoes, quartered

1 large English cucumber, sliced into wedges

½ cup sliced banana peppers

1 small red onion, thinly sliced on the mandolin

Drizzle of good-quality extra-virgin olive oil

Kosher salt

Freshly ground black pepper

This is one of those dishes that I dreamed about for months before I actually made it in real life, but once I did, I was forever in love. It is an homage to one of my favorite dishes—the simple Greek salad. This version is a twist on the classic, one I often describe as a semi-deconstructed version where the vegetables rest on top of a bed of whipped feta. It is not only beautiful in its presentation but also the most refreshing salad on a hot summer day when tomatoes are at their peak.

PREPARE the Whipped Feta and spread it onto a large plate. Arrange the tomatoes, cucumbers, and banana peppers evenly on top of the feta, and sprinkle the red onion slices on top. Finish with a hefty drizzle of olive oil and season with salt and black pepper to taste. Serve immediately.

SOUP SEASON

INTRO

a nourishing broth on a cold winter night.
the perfect soup spoon + the perfect soup bowl.
chilled gazpacho on a warm summer day.
the aroma of a broth simmering on the stove for hours.
leftover soup that's better the next day.

My craving for soups often varies by my mood or the season. I just love that soup can be the ultimate comfort food in the winter and equally soothing and refreshing in the summer. No other staple can be quite as comforting or satisfying as a soup or stew. Think about the power of homemade chicken soup (even just a chicken broth) to soothe a cold. In Mexico, many traditional restaurants will have *caldo* (broth) on the menu all day, which is a testament to it's healing powers. Also, how beautiful is it that you only need a spoon or, in some cases, no utensil at all?

Chicken Soup with Tortellini

SERVES 6

FOR THE CHICKEN SOUP

4-pound whole chicken

3 quarts homemade or high-quality store-bought chicken broth

14 ounces cheese tortellini, preferably fresh

TOPPINGS + ADDITIONS

Any fresh herb, such as flat-leaf parsley, dill, or chives

Shaved Parmesan cheese

Freshly ground black pepper

Pinch of crushed red pepper flakes

For me, there is no dish quite as comforting and satisfying as chicken soup. When I first started cooking in earnest, chicken soup was the first recipe I wanted to master, and it quickly became my go-to in winter. The first day that the temperature would drop, I would rush to the market to buy a whole chicken along with the other ingredients needed to make my favorite soup. One day, on an excursion to gather chicken soup ingredients, I found myself in an Italian specialty store where there were tiny homemade tortellini just begging to be added to the broth. I threw them in and never looked back. While the tortellini turn the soup into a more indulgent treat, they connect me to my Italian roots and to the classic tortellini in brodo that is from the Bologna region in Italy. Although this version it is a bit more homestyle than what you would find in a restaurant, it is the ultimate nourishing comfort food.

To make the broth, I use a nontraditional method that yields an incredibly strong chicken flavor. There are no vegetables like you might find in a traditional chicken noodle soup. Instead, the chicken is cooked in a homemade or high-quality chicken broth to bring out the most incredible, pure, rich chicken flavor.

PLACE the whole chicken into a large, heavy-bottomed pot and add the broth so the chicken is covered, leaving about 1 to 2 inches from the top so that it doesn't overflow. If you don't have enough broth to cover the chicken, you can add water (just be sure to taste and adjust the seasoning after the chicken is cooked and removed). Bring the broth to a gentle simmer over medium heat. Cover, lower the heat to a low simmer, and cook for 1 hour.

TURN OFF the heat and remove the chicken, placing it on a large cutting board; leave the broth in the pot but pass a strainer through it to remove any stray chicken pieces so you have a clean broth. Allow the chicken to cool completely before removing the meat from the bones. I like to give the chicken a rough chop with a knife to help speed the cooling and stop the chicken from cooking. When you are ready to pull the meat off the bones, peel off and discard the skin (or save it for another use). Using your hands, remove all the meat from the bones, discarding any cartilage or tough pieces. Return the meat to the broth.

ADD the tortellini to the broth and cook according to the instructions. Fresh pasta will only take a couple of minutes, but frozen will take longer.

LADLE the soup into bowls and top with herbs, grated Parmesan, black pepper, and crushed red pepper flakes. Serve warm. This will keep for a couple of days in an airtight container in the fridge, or you could also freeze for 2 to 3 months.

Cauliflower Parmesan Soup
with Crisp Pancetta

This is one of those soups that is so simple to make. It has just a few ingredients, but it explodes with flavor. This is always a crowd favorite, and people can never believe how a soup with such complexity is so simple to prepare. The pancetta is optional but is great if you want a little something salty and crunchy to top it off. This is also a great soup to make a double batch of and freeze the leftover because, as a pureed soup, it holds up well. You can then heat it up easily, add the toppings you like, and serve with some bread or a side salad to make a quick meal.

IN A LARGE, HEAVY-BOTTOMED POT, heat the butter and 2 tablespoons olive oil over medium heat. Add the onion and garlic, season with a pinch of salt, and cook until translucent, about 2 minutes.

ADD the cauliflower and 3 tablespoons olive oil and season again with 2 pinches of salt. Cook until the cauliflower is fork tender, around 15 to 20 minutes. When the cauliflower is cooked, add the water or broth, lemon juice, and the Parmesan rind. You want the liquid to cover the cauliflower; if there is not enough, add more until the cauliflower is submerged.

BRING to a boil, then reduce to a simmer and cook for approximately 30 minutes.

WHILE THE SOUP IS COOKING, prepare the toppings and pancetta. Heat about 1 tablespoon olive oil in a medium-sized frying pan over medium heat. Add the pancetta and cook for about 2 minutes on each side until crisp. Set aside on a paper towel–lined plate until you're ready to serve.

REMOVE the Parmesan rind and carefully transfer the soup to a blender. Add the grated Parmesan and cream and blend until super smooth. Taste and adjust the seasoning as necessary. Serve warm with some pieces of the crispy pancetta, a sprinkle of chives, and a drizzle of olive oil. The soup will keep for a couple of days in an airtight container in the fridge or for about 3 months in the freezer.

SERVES 6

3 tablespoons unsalted butter

5 tablespoons extra-virgin olive oil, divided

1 yellow onion, chopped

5 garlic cloves, sliced

Kosher salt

1 head cauliflower, chopped into small florets

4 cups water or a homemade or high-quality store-bought chicken broth

1 lemon, juiced

1 (4 to 5-inch) Parmesan cheese rind

½ cup grated Parmesan cheese

½ cup heavy cream

TOPPINGS + ADDITIONS

4 ounces pancetta

1 to 2 tablespoons minced chives

1 tablespoon extra-virgin olive oil, plus a drizzle for serving

Lentil Soup with Greens + Cumin-Spiced Yogurt

SERVES 6 TO 8

FOR THE SOUP

2 tablespoons extra-virgin olive oil

1 medium yellow onion, finely diced

4 carrots, peeled and finely diced

3 garlic cloves, minced

Kosher salt

Freshly ground black pepper

1 cup green lentils, rinsed and picked through

1 bay leaf

8 cups chicken or vegetable stock, preferably homemade or high-quality store-bought

1 cup loosely packed chopped spinach

1 cup loosely packed chopped kale

FOR THE SPICED YOGURT

1 cup plain whole-milk Greek yogurt

1 tablespoon fresh lemon juice

1 garlic clove, pressed or grated

½ teaspoon ground turmeric

½ teaspoon ground cumin

Kosher salt

Freshly ground black pepper

I love to tell the story of my mom's "hot dog soup." This was actually a lentil soup that she would add sliced hot dogs to in order to coax me and my brother to eat something healthy. I loved that soup so much. I had this ritual where I would eat all the soup around the hot dogs until I was left with just a bowl of sliced hot dog, saving what I thought was the best part for last. In retrospect, I was creating a strong attachment to the lentils by eating the soup this way. When I started making my own homemade lentil soup, I realized how satisfying and hearty lentils were on their own. With some spices, greens, and a swirl of yogurt, the hot dogs were quickly a distant (albeit fond) memory.

IN A LARGE, HEAVY-BOTTOMED POT, heat the olive oil over medium heat. Add the onion, carrots, and garlic; season with salt and pepper, and cook until the vegetables become soft and begin to caramelize, about 15 to 20 minutes. Add the lentils, bay leaf, and stock and bring to a boil.

WHEN THE STOCK BOILS, reduce heat to a simmer and cook until the lentils are tender but still have a little bite to them, about 35 to 40 minutes. Add the spinach and kale and cook until they are wilted and tender, another 2 to 3 minutes.

WHILE THE SOUP IS SIMMERING, make the yogurt. In a small bowl, stir together the ingredients for the yogurt and season with salt and black pepper to taste.

LADLE the soup into bowls and top with a dollop of the spiced yogurt. Serve warm. Both the soup and the yogurt will keep for a few days in an airtight container in the fridge. You can also freeze the soup for up to 3 months.

Tomato Coconut Soup with Lump Crab

Tomato soup has the luxury and adaptability to be both a cold weather comfort food and a warm weather, cool-down indulgence. This version is no exception. In the colder months, you can use canned tomatoes, canned coconut milk, and canned lump crab. In the summer, you can use the freshest, juiciest tomatoes you can find, as well as fresh crab. The crab is totally optional but highly recommended and takes this to another level. Additionally, the particular flavor of coconut is what distinguishes this soup from all the other more traditional tomato soups out there. It gives the soup a sweet undertone that really enhances and pairs perfectly with the crab.

Note: *For ease, I usually use high-quality, canned lump crab meat, which is excellent for this recipe. You could always buy and steam a couple of crab claws and remove the meat, if that is something you have the desire to do. It would be delicious and worth it.*

HEAT the oil and butter in a large saucepan over medium heat. Add the onions, garlic, salt, and crushed red pepper flakes, and cook for a few minutes until the onion and garlic are translucent.

ADD the tomatoes and cook for 10 to 15 minutes, until tender, mashing them a bit with a fork or a potato masher while they're cooking so they release juices and become more of a puree. Once they have cooked down a bit, add the coconut milk. Bring to a slow boil over medium-high heat, then reduce the heat to low, and simmer for another 10 minutes to allow the flavors to develop.

REMOVE from heat and, using a stand blender or immersion blender, blend the soup into a smooth puree. Feel free to add a bit of water if it is too thick. Taste and adjust any seasoning you feel necessary.

IF YOU ARE GOING TO SERVE THIS WARM, transfer the soup back to the pot to keep warm. If you are going to serve cold, transfer it to a container and store in the fridge for several hours or overnight until it's chilled.

MIX the crab and the lime juice in a small mixing bowl using a fork to gently combine, being careful not to break apart the crab too much. Then ladle the soup into bowls and top with the crab and herbs and serve.

SERVES 4

2 tablespoons extra-virgin olive oil

2 tablespoons unsalted butter

1 small yellow onion, sliced

2 garlic cloves, minced

1 teaspoon kosher salt

Pinch of crushed red pepper flakes (optional)

1 (28-ounce) can whole peeled tomatoes or 10 to 12 ripe roma tomatoes, halved

1 (14-ounce) can full-fat unsweetened coconut milk

TOPPINGS+ ADDITIONS

5 ounces lump crab meat (I use a canned lump blue crab)

Juice from 1 lime

Fresh herbs (such as chives, cilantro, or basil), chopped

White Bean + Greens + Sausage Stew with Lemon, Parmesan + Dill

SERVES 2 TO 4

2 to 3 tablespoons extra-virgin olive oil

2 large or 4 small pork or chicken sausages (about 8 ounces), casings removed

1 bunch broccolini, sliced into thin florets and tough stems removed

2 cups kale, stems removed and finely chopped

2 cups spinach, finely chopped

Kosher salt

Freshly ground black pepper

Crushed red pepper flakes

1 tablespoon white wine vinegar

1 (14-ounce) can white beans (I like to use gigante or cannellini)

2 to 3 cups water

1 (2-inch) Parmesan cheese rind

TOPPINGS + ADDITIONS

Lemon

Grated Parmesan cheese

Fresh dill or other herbs

In the colder months, like most people, I crave hearty stews. I often have a particular craving for the combination of sausage and beans. This soup came to me one day when I had some delicious spicy sausage in my fridge begging to be used, as well as some canned beans and a mix of greens. The weather was cold, and I was hungry for a hearty stew, but I had little time to make one. I didn't want to spend the time chopping a lot of onions or other ingredients, so I just started by browning the sausage in hopes that it's intense flavors and the rendered fats would take care of any lack of alliums. Also, I used a Parmesan rind to make up for the lack of broth I had on hand. I couldn't believe how easily, quickly, and perfectly balanced, hearty, and tasty this soup turned out. It has now become my favorite for a quick, flavorful, and filling cold-weather meal.

IN A LARGE, HEAVY-BOTTOMED POT, heat 1 tablespoon olive oil over medium heat. Add the sausage to the pot and cook until browned, about 5 to 7 minutes, all while breaking it into little bits with the back of a fork. Be sure to stir often and scrape any brown bits from the bottom of the pan.

ADD the broccolini and cook for about 3 minutes, until tender. Add the kale and spinach and cook until wilted, about 2 minutes. Season to taste with salt, black pepper, and crushed red pepper flakes. Add the vinegar, and use it to scrape any last brown bits from the bottom of the pan.

ADD the beans with their juices (the juices will add depth to the stew) and just enough water to cover the ingredients. Add the Parmesan rind, lower the heat to a simmer, and cook for approximately 30 minutes to render more flavor.

REMOVE the Parmesan rind, ladle into serving bowls, and serve warm with a squeeze of lemon juice, a dusting of grated Parmesan, and a pinch of dill or another favorite herb.

Potato Leek Soup with Crispy Leeks + Crispy Potatoes

I love adding texture to soup, and a classic potato leek soup felt like the perfect classic base for a layered version. With the crispy leeks and potato crisps on top for an unexpected pop of flavor and crunch, this soup transforms into something that feels more like a meal or perfect lunch served with some toasty bread.

PREHEAT the oven to 450°F. Place the thinly sliced potatoes on a large baking sheet in a single layer (not overlapping), drizzle with olive oil, and season with salt and black pepper. Bake for 10 to 12 minutes, until golden brown and crispy. The potatoes can burn quickly and easily so I suggest checking them every 5 minutes.

HEAT the oil in a large stockpot over medium heat until shimmering (when you drop a piece of leek into the oil to test, it should sizzle). Add ½ cup sliced leeks and cook until they turn golden brown, about 2 to 3 minutes. Be sure to watch carefully and stir often to prevent burning. Remove leeks with a slotted spoon and place on a paper towel–lined plate.

HEAT 2 tablespoons butter and 2 tablespoons olive oil in a large, heavy-bottomed pot over medium heat. Add the additional leek and the garlic and sauté for 2 to 3 minutes until soft. Add the quartered potatoes and chicken broth and bring to a gentle simmer, cooking for approximately 30 minutes or until the potatoes are fork tender.

USING A STAND BLENDER or immersion blender, blend the soup until you have a super-smooth puree. Add in the crème fraîche and blend until incorporated. Taste and adjust seasoning as necessary. Pour or ladle the soup into individual bowls and top with a couple of slices of crispy potato, a pinch of crispy leeks, and some fresh chives or scallions. Serve warm. You can store the soup in an airtight container in the fridge for a few days, or this will freeze well for about 3 months.

SERVES 2 TO 4

FOR THE CRISPY POTATOES

1 medium russet or Idaho potato, peeled and sliced thin on a mandolin

2 tablespoons extra-virgin olive oil

Kosher salt

Freshly ground black pepper

FOR THE CRISPY LEEKS

3 tablespoons vegetable oil

1 large leek, white and pale green parts only, thinly sliced

FOR THE SOUP

2 tablespoons unsalted butter

2 tablespoons extra-virgin olive oil

3 garlic cloves, minced

1 large leek, white and pale green parts only, thinly sliced

2 medium russet or Idaho potatoes, peeled and quartered

4 cups chicken broth (homemade or high-quality store-bought)

½ cup crème fraîche

TOPPINGS + ADDITIONS

Fresh chives or scallions, thinly sliced

Vongole Stew

SERVES 4

2 pounds littleneck clams

3 tablespoons extra-virgin olive oil

5 garlic cloves, minced

1 tablespoon crushed red pepper flakes

1 cup dry white wine, such as sauvignon blanc or pinot gris

6 cups chicken broth

7 ounces capellini or spaghetti, broken in half or quarters

TOPPINGS+ ADDITIONS

½ lemon

1 to 2 tablespoons chopped flat-leaf parsley

You know when you make a vongole pasta and you need to have some delicious crusty bread to sop up every last drop? It's such a delicate sauce that I've always wanted more of, so I created a dish where the pasta and clams are literally swimming in that briny, garlicy broth, making it into more of a stew. This recipe is made using the same basic ingredients you would use to make a vongole pasta, but the only thing that is added is a few cups of broth to give more volume and substance to what I consider an already perfect dish.

SOAK the clams in cold water to clean and release any excess sand.

HEAT the olive oil in a large pot over medium heat. Add the garlic and crushed red pepper flakes and sauté for about 2 minutes, until fragrant. Add the wine and clams to the pot and cook on a low simmer until the clams have opened and the wine has reduced by approximately three-quarters.

AT THIS POINT, you can remove the clams from their shells if you want and add the clam meat to the broth, or you can leave them in their shell. I prefer to serve them in the shell so that it is more of an interactive experience.

ADD the broth and capellini or spaghetti cook for 4 to 5 minutes until al dente (a little more if using spaghetti). Ladle the soup into serving bowls and finish with a squeeze of lemon juice and sprinkle of parsley. Serve warm, immediately.

Golden Salmorejo
(Yellow Tomato Spanish Gazpacho)

Gazpacho is the perfect summertime soup with so many variations. This Spanish version is popular during the hot summer months in Spain. What makes salmorejo slightly different than gazpacho is the addition of bread to the base of the soup for a bit of depth and creaminess. It is traditionally served with a variety of toppings on the side that you can add and customize as you wish. I am taking this one step further and using yellow sungold and yellow heirloom tomatoes in lieu of red tomatoes that are traditionally used because I love their taste as much as I love the vibrant color they lend to this dish.

PLACE all of the ingredients for the soup into a blender and blend on high until super creamy. Taste and make any adjustments to the seasoning as you see fit.

TRANSFER to serving bowls and top with crispy prosciutto or bacon, tomato confit, or whatever other toppings you like. You can also keep this in the fridge in an airtight container and serve it extra cold.

SERVES 4

FOR THE SOUP

2 cups yellow heirloom tomatoes, sliced

1 cup sungold tomatoes

1 (4-inch) piece day-old baguette

1 garlic clove

1 tablespoon minced shallot

1 to 2 teaspoons sherry vinegar

1 teaspoon kosher salt

Freshly ground black pepper

Crushed red pepper flakes

TOPPINGS + ADDITIONS

Crispy prosciutto or bacon

Tomato confit (see How to Confit Any Vegetable, page 197)

Some chopped pickles (banana peppers or guindillas)

Thinly sliced chives or scallions

INTRO

the perfect salty, crunchy potato chip.

popcorn for dinner.

toothpicks as utensils.

blue cheese-stuffed olives and a martini.

snacks for dinner with friends.

I love snacks with a passion. Snacks to me are the edible embodiment of minimal effort for maximum reward and enjoyment. The recipes in this chapter feel a little more like food you would serve for a cocktail or dinner party, but something like fried squash blossoms could also make a perfect lunch for one.

Fried Squash Blossoms with Parmesan + Pomodoro

MAKES 12 SQUASH BLOSSOMS

1 cup high-heat vegetable oil, such as grapeseed or other neutral oil

½ teaspoon kosher salt

1 cup all-purpose flour

½ to 1 cup sparkling water

12 squash blossoms, pistils removed

TOPPING + ADDITIONS

½ cup pomodoro sauce (see Spaghetti Pomodoro with Crispy Basil + Anchovy Breadcrumbs, page 112)

Grated Parmesan cheese

Freshly ground black pepper

When I was growing up, one of my mother's favorite summertime treats for us was to fry up squash blossoms from the garden and serve them with a homemade tomato sauce. Usually she stuffed them with ricotta or goat cheese, but I found the squash blossoms in this recipe to be a much faster, easier way to enjoy beautiful edible flowers. You just give them a quick dunk in the batter, fry, and finish with a sprinkle of Parmesan and a side of tomato sauce (or Salsa Macha, page 194; Garlic Aioli, page 188; Whipped Feta, page 83; or Pesto, page 192). Another unique way you can serve them, which I do often, is wrapped up in a tortilla with some crumbled cheese and salsa.

Some quick tips: *The water-to-flour ratio can vary greatly because of humidity, altitude, and so forth, so add the water a ¼ cup at a time and mix completely until you have a pancake-like batter, or slightly thinner if you want a lighter result. Using sparkling water helps create an airier texture, but feel free to use regular water instead.*

Variations: *To mix it up, try stuffing the squash blossoms with various cheese combinations, such as ricotta and honey or goat cheese and Pesto (page 192).*

IN A LARGE, DEEP FRYING PAN, heat the oil over medium heat. If you are using a thermometer, you want your oil to reach around 350°F. If you don't have a thermometer, you can test when your oil is ready by dropping in a tiny bit of batter—you will know it's ready when the batter sizzles.

WHILE THE OIL IS HEATING, make the batter. In a medium-sized shallow bowl, mix together the salt and flour and then start adding the sparkling water a ¼ cup at a time and mixing to combine. When the batter has a consistency of a thin pancake-like batter, it's ready.

HOLDING THE STEM OF THE BLOSSOM, dredge the flowers in the batter and allow and excess to drop back into the bowl. Drop the dredged flower into the heated oil and fry for about 2 minutes on each side, until crispy and golden. Do this until you've fried all the blossoms, being careful not to overcrowd the pan. Transfer them to a paper towel–lined plate to drain any excess oil before serving.

TRANSFER the blossoms to a serving plate and sprinkle with Parmesan and season with black pepper. Serve with warm pomodoro sauce—or any other sauce of your choice—on the side.

Fried Blue Cheese–Stuffed Olives

I often long for the days when it was common to find blue cheese olives served with a classic martini, so now I prepare and keep them at home as a fun little snack with friends. If you want to take it one step further and fry the olives after they're stuffed with cheese, then you're in for an extra treat. These are also great served with some aioli or spiced yogurt on the side for dipping.

STUFF each olive with the cheese. Then set up the breading station by placing the flour in a shallow bowl, the egg in another bowl, and the panko in a third bowl.

HEAT the oil in a large pan over medium heat until shimmering. Roll each olive first in the flour, then in the egg, then the panko. When all of the olives have been breaded, add them to the heated oil and fry for about 2 minutes, turning halfway through, until golden brown. Remove and place on a paper towel–lined plate. Season with salt and black pepper and serve warm.

MAKES 12 OLIVES

12 green olives (such as Castelvetrano), pits removed

¼ cup crumbled cheese (blue, feta, or goat)

¼ cup all-purpose flour

1 egg, lightly beaten

¼ cup panko breadcrumbs

¼ cup vegetable oil

Kosher salt

Freshly ground black pepper

Feta Dips Three Ways—
Marinated, Baked + Whipped

As you might be able to tell from the recipes in this book, I have a major love affair with feta cheese. One of my favorite pairings for the Whipped Feta is to serve it on a bed of the Tomatoes + Cucumber + Banana Peppers Salad (page 50). Marinated Feta is a new favorite and is an incredibly flavorful dish to serve as an appetizer for a dinner party. And lastly, Baked Feta will always have my heart. I like mine a little spicy, but it can be served so many ways: my two favorites are with some crusty bread for dipping or poured over pasta or rice.

MARINATED

SERVES 4

8-ounce block feta cheese

1 cup good-quality extra-virgin olive oil

SOME MARINATING IDEAS

Garlic, olives, capers, scallion

Sundried tomato, basil

Chiles, garlic, and sesame

COMBINE your marinating ingredients in a small, deep bowl or jar, then whisk in the olive oil. Add the feta block (you can also cut the feta into cubes), ensuring it is mostly covered by the marinade. Transfer to the fridge and allow to sit for at least 2 hours and up to a few days for the feta to absorb the flavors.

continued >>

BAKED

SERVES 4

1 pint cherry tomatoes

1 red chili, seeded and thinly sliced

2 garlic cloves, thinly sliced

2 tablespoons extra-virgin olive oil

Kosher salt

Freshly ground black pepper

8-ounce block feta cheese

TOPPINGS + ADDITIONS

A couple of leaves of torn basil

1 tablespoon chopped parsley

A crusty baguette, sliced sourdough, or crackers for serving

PREHEAT the oven to 400°F. In a small baking dish, add the tomatoes, chili, and garlic. Drizzle with the olive oil, season with salt and pepper, and toss to combine. Nestle the feta in the middle and bake for about 20 minutes. If you want the cheese to be more melted or crispier, change the oven setting to broil and bake it under the broiler for about 2 minutes, until bubbly and golden. Top with the fresh herbs and serve warm, right out of the oven, with bread or crackers.

WHIPPED

IN A FOOD PROCESSOR or powerful blender, add the feta, yogurt, olive oil, lemon juice, and garlic clove and blend until smooth. Season to taste with salt and black pepper. Transfer to a bowl, and finish with the toppings of your choice.

SERVES 4

8 ounces feta cheese

½ cup plain whole-milk Greek yogurt

2 tablespoons extra-virgin olive oil

1 tablespoon fresh lemon juice

1 garlic clove

Kosher salt

Freshly ground black pepper

TOPPINGS + ADDITIONS

A mix of fresh herbs, such as mint, basil, flat-leaf parsley, and dill

Drizzle of extra-virgin olive oil

Spices, such as sumac, Aleppo pepper, crushed red pepper flakes, or chili powder

Pine nuts

Sesame seeds

Roasted vegetables, such as tomatoes, eggplant, or zucchini

Prosciutto-Wrapped Dates with Sundried Tomato + Basil + Goat Cheese

Dates are one of life's sweetest gifts, and they really come alive and show their versatility when paired with salty things. Bacon-wrapped dates are a familiar party food, but I love this retro version with flavors that leave me nostalgic for my childhood. The combination of sundried tomato and goat cheese is the perfect counter to the sweetness of the chewy dates. Somewhere along the way sundried tomatoes lost a bit of their cool, but I think they should have a well-deserved place in the pantry. I particularly love the high-quality ones packed in olive oil.

PREHEAT the oven to 400°F.

STUFF each date with a bit of goat cheese, a sundried tomato, and a basil leaf.

CUT each prosciutto slice into 3 pieces, a little larger than the width of the date. This can vary depending on the size of your prosciutto slices, so judge by measuring with the date. Place the date at the bottom edge of the prosciutto slice and wrap the date into a little package. Place all the wrapped dates onto a baking sheet, drizzle with olive oil, and bake for 10 to 15 minutes, until the prosciutto is crisp and the cheese is melted and bubbly. Serve immediately, warm.

MAKES 12 STUFFED DATES

12 medjool dates, pits removed

6 to 8 ounces goat cheese, softened

12 olive oil–packed sundried tomatoes

12 small fresh basil leaves

4 to 6 slices prosciutto (about 8 ounces)

Drizzle of extra-virgin olive oil

Sautéed Whole Fava Beans
with Mint + Garlic Aioli

SERVES 4

2 tablespoons extra-virgin olive oil

1 pound fava beans, whole (in their pods)

TOPPINGS + ADDITIONS

Juice and zest of 1 lemon

Flaky sea salt

Pinch of crushed red pepper flakes (optional)

2 fresh mint leaves, thinly sliced

Garlic Aioli (page 188)

I love fava beans. Although I love the meditative process of boiling and peeling the beans, it can also be time consuming or tedious to say the least. If you want to enjoy a fava without all that work, then this is the best way to do it. When you eat them this way, sautéed whole, it's a bit like snacking on edamame. When cooked, the skin that you usually remove becomes edible and the pod becomes super tender. Adding some fresh mint and homemade aioli really enhances the whole overall fava snacking experience.

IN A LARGE CAST-IRON PAN, heat the olive oil over medium-high heat. Add the fava beans and sauté for about 2 minutes on each side, until charred.

SPREAD the aioli onto a plate and place the fava beans on top. Finish with the lemon juice and zest, season with salt and the crushed red pepper flakes, and sprinkle the mint on top.

Gilda

If you're familiar with this Spanish tapa from the Basque region, then you know that it's just three simple ingredients arranged on a toothpick or skewer. Despite the simplicity, I had to include this because the intense and incredible flavor of this little bite was my gateway into eating and loving more intense flavors, such as anchovy. It's a perfect example of one of life's simple pleasures. While I was originally overwhelmed by such intense salty and powerful flavors, it is now one of my favorite combinations. Maybe it's the tangy flavor and mild spice of the guindilla pepper or the meatiness of the olive, but this bite is just too perfect not to share and even more perfect to serve at a cocktail hour with aperitifs or martinis.

PUSH one olive onto a skewer, followed by an anchovy and a guindilla pepper. Repeat this with each skewer until all of the ingredients have been skewered. You can do this up to a day in advance and store in the fridge.

MAKES 12

12 skewers or toothpicks, around 3 to 4 inches long

12 green olives, pitted (preferably a smaller variety, and traditionally manzanilla)

6 oil-packed anchovies, sliced in half

12 guindilla peppers

Crispy Butter Beans
+ Pickles + Pepperoni

While crispy beans have been a favorite of mine for a long time, they are often a revelation for friends when I make them in this snack form. The roasted beans have a wonderful crispy texture, the pepperoni adds a little fiery kick, and the pickles add a tangy punch. I strongly suggest using the larger butter beans for this recipe because I think of this as a fun finger-food type of snack. You can easily double or triple this recipe depending on the crowd size you're feeding.

PREHEAT the oven to 400°F.

PLACE the butter beans on a baking sheet and drizzle with olive oil and season with salt and pepper. Roast for 20 to 25 minutes, until the beans are crispy and golden brown. Halfway through, add the pepperoni slices; they will crisp up as well.

REMOVE from the oven and place the butter beans and pepperoni in a shallow serving bowl. Scatter some pickled peppers all around and serve.

SERVES 4

1 (14-ounce) can butter beans (gigante beans), drained and rinsed

Drizzle of extra-virgin olive oil

Kosher salt

Freshly ground black pepper

12 slices pepperoni

12 pickled peppers, such as guindillas

LONG, LEISURELY GATHERINGS

INTRO

tinned fish + butter on toast.

standing around a cheese board + talking for
   hours with friends.

all-day barbecues.

the casual chaos of empty, tossed shells.

beautifully, effortlessly styled spreads made
   for grazing.

an oyster shell as a serving dish.

There are few better ways to entertain yourself and others than with a themed spread of cheese, tinned fish, shellfish, vegetables, cured meats, olives, and any other treats you can think to add. These are just a few examples of my favorite way to create boards and spreads to share. The important thing is to make it as effortless as possible so that you can relax and enjoy the time and conversation with friends and family.

Le Grande Aioli

While this is a classic spread that is served at restaurants and in homes in France, I didn't discover this dream spread until my dear friend, and fellow cookbook author, Susan served it at her house for a dinner party. And it was perfection—just some cut-up vegetables, delicious fresh baked bread, and a large bowl of a homemade aioli (see Garlic Aioli, page 188) to dip it all in. Over the past several years, I try to make a trip to the south of France in summer, and when I get the chance to go to one of my favorite restaurants there, they serve this grand spread. You see it on almost every table, and it is so beautiful and delicious that it is often the main event of the meal. This special dish is always on my table at dinner parties, especially in the summertime when the vegetable spread is particularly bountiful and beautiful.

A FEW OF MY FAVORITE INGREDIENTS FOR THE PERFECT SPREAD

Radishes

Cucumber

Zucchini

Chicories

Fennel

Cherry tomatoes

Green beans

Asparagus

Boiled baby potatoes

Chilled shrimp

Olives

Tinned Fish Spread

The joy of opening a tin of fish that has been preserved in time, from another place, is never lost on me. It always amazes me the power of preservation to create something so special that can feed and nourish you. It can be something that satisfies you as a snack when you have nothing else in your fridge, but it can also be something that's part of a spread to celebrate with friends. When I serve tinned fish as a spread, I like to keep it simple. Open a few cans; serve with crackers and butter, some crusty bread, maybe even some aioli, toothpicks on the side—and go to town. I love it even more when it has a story behind it. I often pick up tinned fish on my travels. It then makes for a conversation piece as well as something delicious to snack on.

SUGGESTED PAIRINGS

Anchovies + Flavored Butter (page 189) + toast

Mussels in escabeche + Garlic Aioli (page 188)

Octopus + Salsa Macha (page 194)

Bocarones + Manchego cheese

Sardines + Dijon mustard + sourdough bread

The Ultimate Cheese Board

It was sometime after college, when I was cooking for myself, that I eventually bought a beautiful cheese board. I would style it with my carefully picked-out ingredients and fill it to the brim. It was also around this time that I discovered that a beautiful balanced cheese board could be one of the best dinners of all time. What could be better than grazing for hours on end with good friends, good conversation, good cheese, and good wine?

With any great cheese board, I am a firm believer that you should stick to three specific types of cheese: salty, spreadable, and stinky. But there is a fourth rule: shape. I think a visual variety makes for a more appealing cheese-board experience. Each cheese should be chosen for its quality, and the same with the other supporting ingredients. I like to only choose 1 or 2 kinds of crackers, 1 crusty baguette, and a few spreads, along with a mustard, something sweet, and olives—always olives. Cured meats can be optional or served on their own separate board, piled high. If you go the meat route, I like to choose 1 hero meat, such as mortadella, salami, or ham.

SOME FAVORITE CHEESES

SALTY	SOFT	STRONG
Parmesan	Brie	Gorgonzola
Asiago	Goat	Blue
Manchego	Burrata	Roquefort
Aged Gouda		

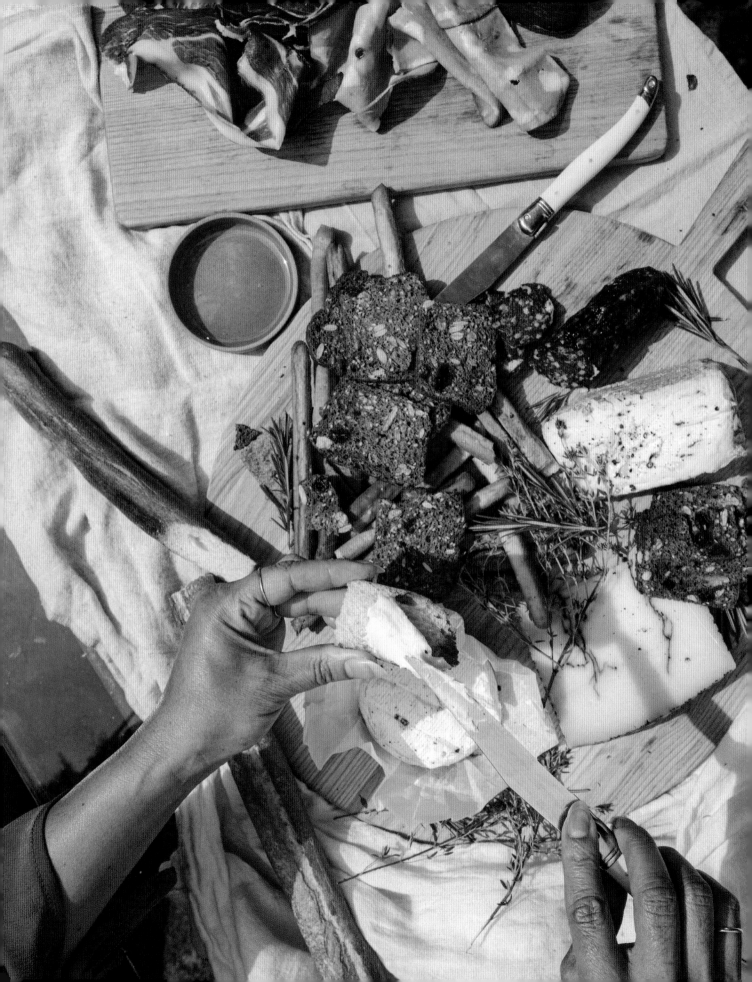

The Ultimate, Classic BBQ Meal: Steak + Sausages with Salad + Chimichurri

One of my all-time favorite summertime meals is an Argentine-style barbecue showcasing a variety of meats, served with a classic, bright, fresh chimichurri and some lightly dressed crisp greens. The beauty of this meal is in its simplicity, highlighting the best meats you can find and using the spread as a canvas to add in other vegetables, fresh breads, or even a cheese board to create the ultimate grazing table.

For the meats, I like to choose one star cut, such as a New York strip, porterhouse, or rib eye, grilled to your liking—for me, it's rare to medium rare, finishing at an internal temperature of 125°F–135°F. The meat gets nothing but a heavy showering of kosher salt a couple of hours before it hits the grill, which helps to tenderize, in addition to seasoning the meat, along with some freshly ground black pepper. I love to add a couple of different types of sausages to the grill as well, to serve alongside the steak. Any fresh sausage that catches your attention will do. Chimichurri (page 192) is the always the perfect complement. Lastly, I like to take some fresh greens, such as a Bibb lettuce or arugula, and dress it very simply with extra-virgin olive oil, lemon juice, salt, and black pepper (see the Arugula Herb Salad with Lemon + Parmesan, page 44). Include potatoes any way you like (Pickle Potato Salad with Crispy Mortadella [page 38] would be particularly wonderful here) or pretty much any recipe from the vegetable or salad chapter of this book.

And, most importantly, a super-delicious full-bodied red wine to round it all out.

The Beauty and Drama of a Whole Grilled Fish

There is something quite elegant and exciting about serving a whole fish. The presentation is effortlessly beautiful and dramatic, and the act of dissecting and eating it in this manner is equally as special. I think it's best to keep it simple by just stuffing the cavity with citrus and herbs, but the sauces and sides are where you can get creative. I think a combination of aioli (see Garlic Aioli, page 188) and fresh herb sauce or salsa (see Chimichurri, page 192, or Salsa Macha, page 194) would be perfect accompaniments. To choose your fish, your local fishmonger should be able to recommend what is fresh and best, but I typically like to look for a small-to-medium-sized, mild-tasting white fish. Red snapper or sea bass are most common and perfect to grill whole.

To prepare your fish, start with a fresh whole fish that has been cleaned and descaled. Pat the fish dry and, inside and outside the cavity, season well with salt and black pepper. Then stuff the cavity with citrus, herbs, and aromatics. I like to use sliced lemon, lime, and/or oranges. Some thinly sliced scallion, ginger, or garlic would also be great additions, as well as some fresh herbs, such as cilantro, dill, or thyme.

Preheat the grill to around 450°F, and cook the fish on each side for 8 to 10 minutes. The outside should be charred and the inside should be cooked through and flake easily with a fork. Serve on a platter with a scattering of herbs, more citrus, and the sauces of your choice.

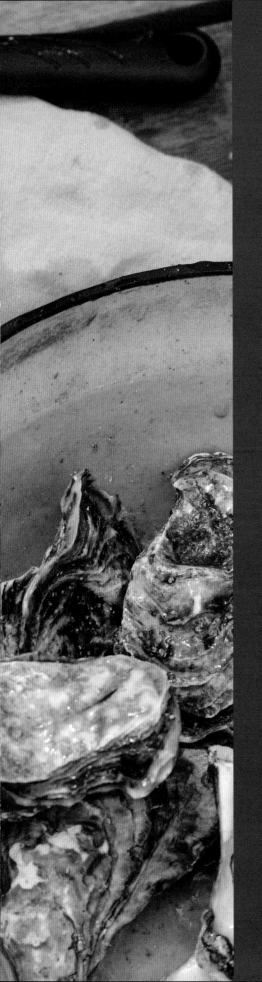

Ode to Oysters

In M.F.K. Fisher's *Consider the Oyster*, she describes oysters and eating an oyster in the most majestic way. The oyster is also spoken about as if it was a person. This book is one of my favorites and really captures the emotions that I feel about the oyster.

Oysters are frequently on my mind. When I eat out and they're on the menu, I will always order a dozen, and it's one of a few things I don't love to share—I typically like to have all 12 to myself. It is also one of my favorite things to serve at dinner parties or pop-ups. While I love oysters with nothing more than just a squeeze of lemon, when I serve mine, I like to make a dressed-up mignonette with the addition of grated ginger and a hint of sesame oil and soy sauce. I also love to add a little topping and texture, such as a crispy shallot or leek. When eating oysters, make sure you scrape out the muscle where it's attached to the shell. It is meaty and delicious and sometimes the best part.

Shellfish Feast

To me, an ultimate simple pleasure is serving a big pot of clams or mussels (or both) cooked in a mixture of butter, alliums, and wine, and served with lots of herbs and—of course—some crusty bread to sop up all the sauce. It's a low-effort, high-reward meal that can make for a beautiful table where you and your guests get to roll up your sleeves, eat with your hands, and make a mess. The finale of empty shells scattered all about is as beautiful as the start.

To steam clams or mussels, there is no need to reinvent the wheel. You can use the same method for both. Start with a big, heavy-bottomed pot. Choose your alliums—I like a mixture of sliced yellow onion, green onion, and a generous several cloves of garlic—and sauté them in about 3 tablespoons each of extra-virgin olive oil and butter. Then add in 2 cups dry white wine, such as sauvignon blanc, and 2 cups chicken broth, bring to a boil, reduce slightly, then add about 2 pounds clams or mussels, well washed. Cook for 7 to 10 minutes, until the shells open.

Serve with a crisp, refreshing white wine—of course, you could and should just use the same wine you cooked them in. On top I like to add a dramatic amount of fresh herbs, such as parsley, dill, or chives. And don't forget the crispy bread and any other things on the side you want to make this a meal. I think Celery Caesar Salad with Bacon Breadcrumbs (page 34) or Layered Salad with Crème Fraîche + Pickle Ranch Dressing (page 45) would also be perfect with this shellfish feast.

PASTA PARTY

INTRO

the twirl of a long pasta on your fork.
tomato sauce cooking for hours on the stove.
a snowy mound of freshly grated parmsean.
rodka sauce with extra vodka.
sunday supper, sunday sauce.
bolognese nights with friends.

Pasta is my heart, my true love, my greatest of all comfort food. Growing up with grandparents who came from Italy, I was blessed with fresh pasta and homemade tomato sauce on a weekly basis. My grandmother's greatest joy was feeding me and the family, but she especially appreciated my insatiable appetite for pasta. Growing up this way instilled in me a deep love and appreciation for quality ingredients and patience in the cooking process. Whenever asked what I would want as my last meal, it is, without hesitation, a perfect bowl of pasta. These are some of my tried-and-true favorites that I have made over and over again through the years. Some of my most cherished recipes.

Spaghetti Pomodoro with Crispy Basil + Anchovy Breadcrumbs

SERVES 6

FOR THE PASTA + SAUCE

2 tablespoons plus ¼ cup extra-virgin olive oil, divided

4 tablespoons unsalted butter, divided

1 large yellow onion, diced

Kosher salt

Freshly ground black pepper

8 garlic cloves: 4 minced, 4 smashed, divided

28 ounces canned whole peeled tomatoes, ideally San Marzano

12 fresh basil leaves

Crushed red pepper flakes

½ cup grated Parmesan cheese, plus more for topping

2 tablespoons kosher salt

1 pound spaghetti

FOR THE ANCHOVY BREADCRUMBS

1 garlic clove

2 anchovy filets

1 tablespoon crushed red pepper flakes

½ teaspoon kosher salt

2 tablespoons extra-virgin olive oil

1 cup panko breadcrumbs

This is quite possibly one of my most favorite things to eat and make. If I want to celebrate something, I will make this dish. If I am having a bad day and need a pick me up, I will make this dish. It's my ultimate comfort, happy food. This is a very simple tomato sauce that maximizes just a few ingredients to get loads of flavor. It's my go-to tomato sauce that I use for a simple pasta but also for any dish that calls for a tomato sauce. I almost always make a double batch when I am making this, and I freeze the leftovers so I always have some on hand. It has a double hit of basil—cooked into the sauce and as a crispy garnish—that, along with the anchovy breadcrumbs, really puts this simple pasta and sauce in a league of its own.

TO PREPARE THE SAUCE, heat 2 tablespoons olive oil and 2 tablespoons butter in a large, deep saucepan over medium heat. Add the onion and a hefty pinch of salt and cook for 15 to 20 minutes, until the onion starts to become golden brown and is beginning to caramelize. Add the 4 minced garlic cloves and cook until fragrant, another 2 to 3 minutes. Add the tomatoes and 2 pinches of salt and some black pepper to season and cook 20 to 30 minutes, smashing the tomatoes every so often, until they have cooked down and become more of a sauce.

WHILE THE TOMATOES ARE COOKING, heat a small frying pan over medium-low heat. Add ¼ cup olive oil, the basil leaves, the 4 smashed garlic cloves, and a pinch of crushed red pepper flakes. Gently fry the basil until the edges are crisp, about 2 minutes. Carefully remove the basil with tongs and set onto a paper towel–lined plate. You will use these as garnish later. Reserve the oil you cooked them in for the next step. You can save the garlic for another use or add it to the sauce if you like extra garlic flavor.

USING A FOOD MILL, puree the tomato sauce over a bowl, leaving behind the seeds and skins. Wipe clean the pan used for the sauce, and strain the oil from the basil leaves into the pan. Return the pureed tomato sauce to the pan with the oil. Continue to cook the tomato sauce on a very low simmer while you cook the breadcrumbs.

PLACE the garlic, anchovy, crushed red pepper flakes, and salt into a mortar and pestle. Smash the mixture until you have a paste.

HEAT 2 tablespoons olive oil in a small frying pan over medium-low heat. Add the anchovy paste and cook for 2 minutes, until fragrant. Then add the panko and toast for about 2 minutes, stirring to prevent burning, until golden brown. Set aside.

TO PREPARE THE PASTA, fill a large pot with water, add 2 tablespoons salt, and bring to a boil over high heat. Add the pasta and cook until al dente. Then, using tongs, transfer the pasta to the saucepan along with the Parmesan and the remaining 2 tablespoons butter. Stir, shake, and toss to coat the pasta with the sauce and until the Parmesan and butter have dissolved into the sauce. Plate the pasta in individual bowls and top with breadcrumbs, grated Parmesan, and crispy basil leaves to serve.

Not-So-Classic Bolognese

Of all the dishes I have made over the years, this one might be the one that brings together and bonds my friends and family the most. There are a couple of things I have tweaked over the (many) years I have been lovingly cooking this dish, making this slightly different from a typical Bolognese. The most obvious is I've broken up the holy trinity of Italian cooking by leaving out the carrots and celery, using instead just onion and garlic. I did this because I wanted the meat to shine and for each flavor of each ingredient to really stand out. I also use a dry white wine (as opposed to the more traditional rich red) because its bright, tart flavor is a perfect contrast to the richness of the meat.

IN A MEDIUM SAUCEPAN, heat 2 tablespoons butter and the olive oil over medium heat. Add the onion and cook for 15 to 20 minutes, until the onions are soft, golden brown, and beginning to caramelize. Add the garlic and cook until fragrant, another 2 minutes. Then add the ground beef and pork, season well with salt and black pepper while stirring and breaking apart the meat until it is cooked through and no longer pink. Add the milk and lower the heat to medium-low and cook until the milk has evaporated, about 7 to 10 minutes. Add the wine and simmer, stirring occasionally, until the wine is about 95 percent evaporated, about 5 to 7 minutes. Then add the tomatoes, smashing and breaking them apart with a spoon to make them into more of a puree. Reduce heat to a very low, lazy simmer. Cook, uncovered, for 2 to 3 hours, stirring occasionally. If it gets too dry and is sticking, add a splash of water. About halfway through, taste and add additional salt and pepper if necessary.

WHEN YOU'RE READY TO SERVE, prepare the pasta. Bring a large pot of water to a boil along with about 2 tablespoons salt. Add the pasta and cook for 2 minutes less than the suggested time on the package. Transfer the cooked pasta to the Bolognese pan, add the remaining tablespoon of butter, and finish cooking the pasta in the sauce, while stirring, until the pasta is al dente, about 2 to 3 minutes. Plate and top with Parmesan, basil, and parsley, and serve immediately, warm.

SERVES 4 TO 6

3 tablespoons unsalted butter, divided

2 tablespoons extra-virgin olive oil

1½ cups yellow onion, sliced

5 to 7 garlic cloves, minced

1 pound ground beef, 80 percent lean

½ pound ground pork

Kosher salt

Freshly ground black pepper

1 cup whole milk

1 cup dry white wine, such as sauvignon blanc or pinot gris

1 (28-ounce) can Italian plum tomatoes with their juices

1½ pounds pasta (long, flat noodles such as pappardelle, or a short pasta such as rigatoni)

TOPPINGS + ADDITIONS

Grated Parmesan cheese

Fresh basil leaves, torn

Flat-leaf parsley, chopped

Gnocchi with Lemon-Spinach Ricotta

SERVES 4

2 cups loosely packed spinach

Juice from 1 lemon

8 fresh basil leaves

1 garlic clove, smashed

¼ cup grated Parmesan cheese

¼ cup whole-milk ricotta

½ teaspoon kosher salt

Freshly ground black pepper

1 to 2 tablespoons extra-virgin olive oil

1 pound gnocchi

TOPPINGS + ADDITIONS

Freshly ground black pepper

Lemon zest

Grated Parmesan cheese

Basil leaves, torn

I am in love with the vibrant green color of this dish. Just seeing this sauce draped over the pillows of gnocchi makes me want to dive right in and devour it. This sauce has a bit of a pesto vibe, without the nuts, and because creamy ricotta gets blended in, the result is a velvety smooth sauce that is so tasty and luscious you will want to sop up every last drop. As an added bonus, this pasta makes excellent leftovers. While this recipe calls for store-bought gnocchi (for ease), of course you're welcomed and encouraged to make your own fresh gnocchi for this as well.

FILL a large bowl with ice water and have it nearby. Bring a large pot of water to a boil. Add the spinach and cook for about 2 minutes, until wilted. Remove from the boiling water and transfer to the ice bath, then squeeze as much excess water from the spinach as you can and transfer it to a blender. Add the lemon juice, basil leaves, garlic, Parmesan, and ricotta to the blender with the spinach and season with salt and black pepper. Blend until you have a super-smooth consistency. You can add 1 to 2 tablespoons olive oil while the blender is running to help thin out the texture.

BOIL the gnocchi until cooked and tender and floating to the surface. When the gnocchi is done, drain it from the water and transfer to a serving plate or bowl.

TO SERVE, pour the sauce over the gnocchi and top with more black pepper, lemon zest, Parmesan, and some torn basil leaves.

Pork Chorizo Ragu with Caramelized Fennel + Shallots

SERVES 4

3 tablespoons unsalted butter, divided

2 tablespoons extra-virgin olive oil

1 fennel bulb, thinly sliced, fronds reserved

3 shallots, sliced

3 garlic cloves, minced

Kosher salt

Freshly ground black pepper

½ pound ground pork

½ pound fresh chorizo or other sausage, casings removed

1 pound pasta

½ cup dry white wine, such as sauvignon blanc or pinot gris

½ cup grated Parmesan cheese

TOPPINGS + ADDITIONS

Grated Parmesan cheese

Crushed red pepper flakes

Fennel fronds

Flat-leaf parsley (optional)

White ragu is a delicious and lighter spin on the more traditional "red" ragu. The stars of this sauce are the sausage, white wine, shallots, and fennel—their flavors really get a chance to shine. Fennel and sausage always pair perfectly and in this dish they especially stand out and enhance each other. While I love the addition of the chorizo for extra spice and a flavor kick, feel free to use any fresh sausage you prefer.

IN A LARGE PAN, heat 2 tablespoons butter and olive oil over medium heat. Add the fennel, shallots, and garlic, season with salt and pepper, and cook for about 10 minutes, until they're super soft, turning golden brown, and beginning to caramelize. Then add the ground pork and the chorizo. Cook, while stirring and breaking apart any larger chunks, until the meat is cooked and has broken down into smaller pieces, about 7 to 10 minutes.

BRING a large pot of water to a boil, add the pasta, and cook until al dente. When the pasta is cooking, add the wine to the ragu and cook it down until it's almost all reduced but has created a saucier texture, about 3 to 5 minutes.

USING TONGS, transfer the cooked pasta to the ragu with about ½ cup pasta water, along with the remaining 1 tablespoon butter and the Parmesan. Toss the pasta with the ragu so the sauce starts to coat the noodles.

TRANSFER the pasta to bowls or plates and top with more Parmesan, crushed red pepper flakes, fennel fronds, and parsley.

Eggplant + Red Onion
+ Burrata Pasta

Onion is one of my very favorite pasta ingredients. I would go so far as to say that onions are underrated and underutilized as the main *ingredient of most pasta dishes. Melty, caramelized onions add such a great depth of flavor and texture to pasta. This simple recipe does not have a hearty sauce, so it relies more heavily on the onion to create that depth and extra umami.*

HEAT 2 tablespoons olive oil and 2 tablespoons butter in a large frying pan over medium heat. Add the eggplant and sauté for 7 to 10 minutes, until soft and golden brown. You might need to add a bit more oil so that the eggplant doesn't stick. Once the eggplant is cooked, transfer it to a plate while you cook the onion.

HEAT the remaining 2 tablespoons olive oil and 2 tablespoons butter in the same large frying pan and add the onion. Cook for 15 to 20 minutes, until the onion cooks down and begins to caramelize. Add the eggplant to the onions and stir to incorporate. Remove from the heat while you cook the pasta.

BRING a large pot of water with 2 tablespoons salt to a boil. Add the pasta and cook until al dente. Place the pan with the onion and eggplant over low heat and, using tongs, transfer the pasta to the onion and eggplant. Add 2 tablespoons pasta water to the sauce and give the pan a few tosses and shakes to coat the pasta. Tear the burrata into pieces and add to the pasta, then add some grated Parmesan and toss and shake a few more times to incorporate. Transfer the pasta to serving bowls, and finish with a little more Parmesan and the torn basil.

SERVES 4 TO 6

4 tablespoons extra-virgin olive oil, divided

4 tablespoons unsalted butter, divided

1 large eggplant, cubed

1 small red onion, sliced

1 pound short pasta, such as rigatoni or paccheri

8 ounces burrata cheese

Grated Parmesan cheese

A few fresh basil leaves, torn

Crab + Sungold Tomato Pasta

SERVES 4

2 tablespoons unsalted butter

2 tablespoons extra-virgin olive oil

1 large shallot, minced

5 garlic cloves, minced

1 quart sungold tomatoes, halved

Kosher salt

Freshly ground black pepper

Crushed red pepper flakes

½ pound lump crab meat

Juice from 1 lemon

1 pound long pasta, such as spaghetti, bucatini, or linguini

When I lived in Florida, there was an Italian restaurant that I would frequent with my close friends. About once a week, we would sit at the bar there and order the crab pasta. There are few restaurant dishes I have craved as much as this one. It has been years since I have been to that restaurant, but I still dream about that pasta all the time, so naturally I had to create my own version. There is something about the way that the lump crab melts into the pasta, giving the illusion that there is cream in the pasta, but the only dairy is butter. While you can use red cherry tomatoes, I love to make this with beautiful, ripe sungold tomatoes to give it a sunny, happy hue.

HEAT the butter and oil in a large pan over medium heat. Add the shallot and garlic and cook for 1 to 2 minutes, until soft. Add the tomatoes and season with salt, black pepper, and a couple of pinches of crushed red pepper flakes, and cook while stirring to keep the shallots and garlic from burning. After about 2 minutes, when the tomatoes are tender, turn the heat to a low simmer and smash them with a fork or masher (do this gently so they don't burst and make a mess!) until it becomes thick and saucy.

WHILE THE TOMATOES ARE GENTLY SIMMERING, place the crab in a small bowl and mix with the lemon juice. Add the crab to the sauce and stir until the crab dissolves into the tomatoes. Remove from the heat temporarily while you prepare the pasta, so the sauce does not reduce too much.

BRING a large pot of water to a boil and add 2 tablespoons salt. Cook the pasta until al dente. Return the sauce to a low-heat simmer about 2 minutes before the pasta is ready. Once the pasta is al dente, use tongs to transfer it, along with ½ cup pasta water, to the sauce and vigorously toss the pasta until it is coated and the sauce thickens a bit. Transfer to bowls and serve with some additional crushed red pepper flakes if you want some extra spice.

DINNERTIME

INTRO

sobremesa (the time spent talking at the table with friends after the meal has ended).

dreaming about what to make for dinner while you're eating lunch (or breakfast).

crispy chicken skin shared plates, family style.

leftovers.

a perfectly cooked steak.

Dinner is my most treasured and sacred meal. It is a meal I will never skip, and it is something I love to celebrate whether is for just myself or a full house. While I am someone who loves to eat out for ease or excitement and inspiration, if given the option I will almost always choose eating in. I have several recipes in my arsenal that I reach for—whether it is for a healthy night in for me, plus one or two more, or for a crowd—and these are some of my most cherished and most made.

Lamb Meatballs with Mint-Pistachio Pesto + Lemon Labneh

SERVES 4

FOR THE LAMB MEATBALLS

1 egg

½ cup panko breadcrumbs

½ teaspoon ground cumin

Crushed red pepper flakes (optional)

1 tablespoon flat-leaf parsley, chopped

1 tablespoon cilantro, chopped

2 tablespoons extra-virgin olive oil

2 teaspoons kosher salt

2 garlic cloves, pressed or grated

1 pound ground lamb

FOR THE MINT-PISTACHIO PESTO

2 cups fresh mint leaves

1 cup flat-leaf parsley

½ cup unsalted, shelled pistachios

1 garlic clove

Juice from ½ lemon

1 teaspoon kosher salt

Freshly ground black pepper

½ cup extra-virgin olive oil

FOR LEMON LABNEH

1 cup labneh, or plain whole-milk Greek yogurt

Zest and juice from 1 lemon

Kosher salt

Freshly ground black pepper

TOPPINGS + ADDITIONS

1 head Bibb lettuce, leaves separated

A few pieces of warm pita bread

When I was growing up, meatballs made a weekly appearance on my grandmother's dinner table. Being Italian, she always served them with red sauce. While her more traditional version of spaghetti and meatballs will always be one of my all-time favorites, this variation has a special place in my heart because it feels like a lighter, fresher, and totally different take on how to serve meatballs. I have made these many times for dinner parties as well as for events to feed a crowd because it's easy to make a large batch—just make the meatballs a few hours in advance and pop them into the oven when you're ready to serve. I like to serve this with a large plate of Bibb lettuce, so you can make little meatball-lettuce tacos if you want. I also think some warm pita would be a welcomed addition.

PREHEAT the oven to 425°F.

IN A LARGE BOWL, lightly beat the egg and then add in the panko, cumin, crushed red pepper flakes, parsley, cilantro, olive oil, salt, and garlic and stir to combine. Add in the lamb and stir to incorporate all the ingredients.

ROLL 1 to 2 tablespoons of the lamb mixture between your hands to form a ball, and transfer to a parchment-lined baking sheet. Repeat until all the meatballs have been formed.

BAKE the meatballs until brown and cooked through, about 10 minutes.

WHILE THE MEATBALLS ARE COOKING, prepare the pesto and labneh. In a food processor or blender, add the mint, parsley, pistachios, garlic, lemon juice, salt, and black pepper. Pulse to combine. Then, while the food processor is running, add the olive oil until you have a smooth consistency.

IN A SMALL MIXING BOWL, add the labneh, lemon zest and juice, salt, and black pepper, and stir to combine.

TRANSFER the meatballs to a serving plate. Dollop the pesto and labneh into individual serving bowls, or alternatively you can spread the labneh onto the plate and arrange the meatballs on top with the pesto drizzled over the meatballs. Arrange the Bibb lettuce leaves and the pita bread onto a large plate, and serve.

Salmon Puttanesca

I have a couple of salmon recipes that are my go-to for those nights when I want to make something nourishing yet fun and delicious. This recipe checks off all those boxes and is quite simple to make. Full of all my favorite flavors—salty capers, briny olives, and anchovies—it's no surprise that this one of my staple recipes.

TO PREPARE THE PASTE for the sauce, place the minced garlic and anchovies on a cutting board and mince them until you create a very smooth paste. Add the oregano and crushed red pepper flakes and mince them in as well. Transfer the paste to a bowl and stir in 4 tablespoons vegetable oil, and set aside.

PAT the salmon dry and season lightly with salt and black pepper. Heat 2 tablespoons vegetable oil in a large cast-iron pan (enough to coat the bottom of the pan) over medium-high heat. The pan should be hot enough so that the salmon sizzles when it hits the pan. Add the salmon, skin side down, cook for 2 to 3 minutes, flip, and then cook for 2 more minutes. Transfer the salmon to a plate while you cook the tomato sauce.

USING THE SAME PAN and oil you just cooked the salmon in, lower the heat to medium low, and add the anchovy-garlic paste. Cook for approximately 1 minute while stirring, until fragrant. Add the tomato paste and cook for another 1 to 2 minutes. Add the water and stir until everything is combined. Next, add the capers, olives, and lemon juice. Taste and season if necessary. Lastly, add the salmon back to the pan. Cover and cook for 4 minutes for medium rare or 8 minutes for medium well. Transfer the salmon to serving plates along with the sauce and finish with the garnishes of your choice.

SERVES 2

5 garlic cloves, minced

3 oil-packed anchovy filets

2 teaspoons dried oregano

1/4 teaspoon crushed red pepper flakes

6 tablespoons vegetable oil, such as sunflower or grapeseed, divided

2 (8-ounce) skin-on salmon filets

Kosher salt

Freshly ground black pepper

2 tablespoons tomato paste

1/2 cup water

2 tablespoons capers

1/2 cup kalamata olives, pitted and halved

1 tablespoon fresh lemon juice

TOPPINGS + ADDITIONS

Fresh lemon Juice

Lemon slices

Chopped fresh flat-leaf parsley

Minced fresh chives

Crispy Baked Beans + Fish + Olive Relish

SERVES 2

1 (14-ounce) can gigante or cannellini beans, drained

¼ cup extra-virgin olive oil

½ lemon, thinly sliced

2 to 3 garlic cloves, crushed

1 to 2 pinches crushed red pepper flakes

Kosher salt

Freshly ground black pepper

2 (6-to-8-ounce) filets cod, sea bass, or other thin, white fish

FOR THE RELISH

10 green olives (preferably cerignola or Castelvetrano), pitted and minced

1 serrano or jalapeño chili, seeded and minced

1 garlic clove, grated or pressed

Kosher salt

Freshly ground black pepper

Juice from ½ lemon (use the other ½ lemon from the beans)

¼ cup extra-virgin olive oil

Who doesn't love a delicious one-pan dish? Crispy beans are always such a treat, and they pair so well with a mild white fish and this olive relish. This recipe is extremely flexible and forgiving as you can use any kind of bean or fish combination that you want, just keeping in mind that it might affect the cooking time (a longer cooking time if you use a thicker cut of fish). Lastly, if olives or olive relish aren't your thing, you can top this fish with any kind of condiment your heart desires. A Chimichurri (page 192), romesco, or a salsa all would be great with this simple fish.

PREHEAT the oven to 425°F.

PLACE the beans in a small baking dish, drizzle with enough olive oil to cover the bottom of the pan, and slightly submerge the beans. Then add the lemon slices, garlic, crushed red pepper flakes, and season with salt and pepper. (Make sure your crushed garlic is submerged in the oil to prevent it from burning.) Bake for 15 to 25 minutes, until the beans are crisp to your liking.

MEANWHILE, pat the fish dry and season with salt and pepper. Once the beans are crisped, remove from the oven, lay the seasoned fish on top of the beans, and drizzle a little olive oil over the fish. Cook for another 7 to 10 minutes. (This all depends on your oven and the thickness of your fish, so check it after 7 minutes, and cook more if need be. It should be cooked through and easily flaked with a fork.)

WHILE THE FISH IS BAKING, make your relish. In a small bowl, add all of the ingredients for the relish and stir to combine.

ONCE THE FISH IS DONE, transfer to a serving platter and serve with the relish on the side or spooned on top of the fish and beans.

Sesame Chicken Milanese with Crunchy Radish-Herb Slaw

If I had to list my most beloved classic foods, chicken Milanese would be high on that list for sure. It needs little introduction: it's the ultimate comfort food. I love to pair it with a fresh, crunchy salad or slaw to contrast with the richness of the crispy, nutty crust. I also think an extra little serving of mayonnaise and spicy mustard on the side is a must. This version has sesame seeds for some extra crunch and texture.

IN A LARGE BOWL, stir together the mayonnaise, lemon juice, salt, and black pepper. Add in the cabbage, radishes, scallions, cilantro, and mint and toss to combine. Set aside (or in the fridge) while you prepare the chicken.

IN A LARGE, SHALLOW BOWL, combine the panko, flour, lemon zest, sesame seeds, garlic powder, salt, and black pepper. Be sure to have the beaten eggs in a bowl nearby. In a large frying pan, heat the oil over medium heat for 2 to 3 minutes. It's ready when you drop a bit of batter in and it sizzles. Dredge your chicken in the egg and then in the flour mixture and place it straight into the hot pan. Do this with the second piece of chicken. Cook for 2 to 3 minutes on each side, until golden brown. Transfer the chicken to a serving plate, give it a squeeze of lemon, season with some salt, and then place a mound of the slaw on top and serve with lemon wedges, and some mayonnaise, aioli, or mustard on the side.

SERVES 4

FOR THE SLAW
½ cup mayonnaise

Juice from 1 lemon

½ teaspoon kosher salt

Freshly ground black pepper

1 cup purple cabbage, shredded

4 radishes, thinly sliced

3 scallions, thinly sliced

1 large handful fresh cilantro, chopped

4 or 5 fresh mint leaves, chopped

FOR THE CHICKEN
½ cup panko breadcrumbs

½ cup all-purpose flour

Zest from 1 lemon

¼ cup sesame seeds

½ teaspoon garlic powder

½ teaspoon kosher salt

Freshly ground black pepper

2 eggs, lightly beaten

¼ cup vegetable oil

4 boneless, skinless chicken breasts, pounded to a ¼-inch thickness

TOPPINGS + ADDITIONS
Lemon wedges

Mayonnaise or aioli, for dipping

Dijon or whole-grain mustard, for dipping

Pickle-Brined Sheet-Pan Chicken with Capers, Red Onion + Dill

My love for pickle juice knows no bounds, and this is one of my favorite ways to use it and all its glory—plus, this chicken dish has been a longtime favorite go-to weeknight meal. The chicken gets a brine bath a few hours before roasting, then gets basted in that same pickle brine as it's cooking. In the end, that brine turns into a tangy sauce of sorts for the finished dish. The pickle juice is there to tenderize the meat and impart a slightly tangy taste to the roasted chicken. This dish is perfect served over some rice or a grain, and you could also add other vegetables to the pan when roasting. It's a perfect canvas to get creative and make a hearty, delicious meal.

SEASON the chicken with salt, pepper, and cumin. Place the chicken in a resealable plastic bag and pour in the pickle juice. Allow it to brine either overnight or for at least 1 hour.

PREHEAT the oven to 450°F. Scatter the sliced red onion all around a medium sized baking sheet and drizzle the olive oil over the onion and season with salt and pepper. Remove the chicken from the brine, place on the baking sheet with the onion, and pat the chicken skin dry to ensure a crispy skin. Pour the remaining brine around the onions. Bake for 15 minutes, then baste the chicken with the released juices and add the capers. Return to the oven and bake for another 10 to 15 minutes, until the skin is golden brown and an instant read thermometer reads 165°F.

TRANSFER the chicken to a serving platter, scatter the red onion and capers all around the chicken, and spoon any leftover sauce and rendered chicken fat over the top. Finish with a handful of chopped dill and serve.

SERVES 4 TO 6

4 to 6 pieces bone-in, skin-on chicken (I prefer a mix of thighs and drumsticks)

Kosher salt

Freshly ground black pepper

1 teaspoon ground cumin

2 cups juice from any kind of pickle, preferably dill pickle or a jalapeño for spice

1 red onion, sliced into wedges

2 to 3 tablespoons of extra-virgin olive oil

2 tablespoons capers

1 handful fresh dill, chopped

Sheet-Pan Eggplant Parm/Lasagna

SERVES 2

1 large eggplant, sliced into ¼-inch-thick pieces lengthwise

Extra-virgin olive oil

Kosher salt

Freshly ground black pepper

8 ounces whole-milk ricotta

½ cup grated Parmesan cheese

1 large egg

2 cups jarred or homemade pomodoro sauce

6 to 8 no-boil lasagna noodles

8 ounces mozzarella cheese, sliced

TOPPINGS + ADDITIONS

Torn fresh basil leaves

Both lasagna and eggplant Parmesan are two classic dishes I adore and grew up eating all the time. However, both dishes require a labor of love in the kitchen, and sometimes I just don't have the time to make them. This version I came up with is much easier to make, and you get to have the best of both worlds. It is comprised of layers of eggplant and layers of noodles that will satisfy all the cravings for both of those more traditional dishes. While you can use a good-quality jarred sauce to make this recipe, I would suggest going a step further and making a pomodoro sauce (see Spaghetti Pomodoro with Crispy Basil + Anchovy Breadcrumbs, page 112) for extra depth of flavor.

PREHEAT the oven to 400°F.

LINE a large sheet pan with parchment paper. Place the eggplant onto the sheet pan, brush both sides generously with olive oil, and season with salt and pepper. Bake until the eggplant is tender, 10 to 12 minutes. Place the eggplant on a plate and set the pan aside.

WHILE THE EGGPLANT IS BAKING, prepare the cheese mix. In a medium bowl, mix the ricotta, Parmesan, and egg until thoroughly combined. Season with a pinch of salt and black pepper.

USING THE SAME PARCHMENT-LINED PAN you cooked the eggplant on, spoon a bit of the pomodoro sauce onto the bottom, right in the middle of the pan (a little larger than the slices of eggplant), then start to layer the eggplant, noodles, and cheese. Place a slice of eggplant on top of the sauce. Then add a layer of cheese mixture, then the noodle, and then sauce. Do this until you have stacked all the eggplant and noodles. Add the sliced mozzarella on top.

RETURN to the oven and bake until the noodles are tender, and the cheesy is bubbly and golden brown, about 20 minutes. Remove from the oven and allow to sit for about 5 minutes. Serve warm, topped with torn basil leaves.

Shrimp Scampi + Tomato Rice

SERVES 2

FOR THE TOMATO RICE

5 roma tomatoes

3 garlic cloves

2 tablespoons extra-virgin olive oil

2 tablespoons unsalted butter

Kosher salt

1 cup jasmine or basmati rice

2 cups water

FOR THE SHRIMP SCAMPI

12 shrimp, with shell on and heads intact

2 cups dry white wine, preferably sauvignon blanc

3 tablespoons unsalted butter

3 tablespoons extra-virgin olive oil

8 garlic cloves, thinly sliced

1 to 2 tablespoons crushed red pepper flakes

Kosher salt

Freshly ground black pepper

Juice from 1/2 lemon

TOPPINGS + ADDITIONS

Lemon wedges

1 large handful fresh herbs of your choice (such as flat-leaf parsley, chives, or dill), chopped

If I see shrimp scampi on a menu, it is a foregone conclusion—I will order it. Because of my love for this retro dish, I wanted to create my own updated spin on its classic flavor profile. This is a dish that I have made almost weekly for the past few years, and I love my ritual of going to the fish market, picking out fresh shrimp, and then selecting a delicious bottle of wine to go into the sauce—as well as my wine glass when I am cooking. A good-tasting, dry white wine is super important to create the perfect balance in a scampi. I also take it one step further by reducing the wine with the shrimp shells to enhance the overall flavor. With this version, I love to serve a tomato-laced rice as the perfect accompaniment to absorb and highlight the garlicky scampi sauce.

Note: *I prefer to use larger shrimp for this recipe, and I like to cook them with the head on—for flavor and presentation. However, if head-on shrimp are not for you, or if you cannot find them, any large shrimp variety (with peels) will do—around 16/20 count (per pound).*

GRATE the tomatoes on a box grater into a bowl. Using a microplane, grate the garlic into the same bowl. Pour in the olive oil and stir to combine.

HEAT the butter in a small pot over medium heat. Add the tomatoes and garlic, season with salt, and cook for 2 minutes, until fragrant. Add the rice and cook and stir for another minute. Next, add the water, bring to a boil, cover, and reduce the heat to a simmer. Cook for 20 minutes, until the rice is tender. Remove from heat and set aside, covered, while you prepare the shrimp.

PEEL the shrimp by only removing the middle part of the shell, keeping the head and tail intact. Place the shrimp shells in a small saucepan, then add the wine. Bring the pan to a gentle simmer over medium heat and cook to reduce the wine by half (leaving approximately 1 cup). Strain the wine from the shells and set the wine aside to use to make the scampi sauce.

HEAT the butter and oil in the same pan over medium heat. Add the garlic and crushed red pepper flakes and cook for 2 minutes, until the garlic is fragrant. Add the reserved wine and allow it all to reduce again by half.

ADD the shrimp, season with salt and pepper, and sauté until pink and cooked through, about 2 minutes per side, depending on the size of your shrimp. Be careful not to overcook the shrimp. Just before they're done, squeeze the lemon juice over the shrimp.

SPOON the rice onto a large serving dish, place the shrimp on top, and pour the remaining sauce all over the shrimp and rice. Finish with a scattering of herbs and some extra lemon wedges on the side.

Crispy-Skin Chicken Breast + Ginger-Scallion Sauce

SERVES 2

FOR THE GINGER-SCALLION SAUCE

¼ cup scallions, thinly sliced

1 garlic clove, grated or minced

1 (1-inch) piece fresh ginger, grated

1 jalapeño or serrano chili, seeded and minced

¼ cup vegetable oil, such as sunflower or grapeseed

1 teaspoon soy sauce or tamari

½ teaspoon sesame oil

½ teaspoon kosher salt

FOR THE CHICKEN BREASTS

2 (8-ounce) skin-on, boneless chicken breasts

Kosher salt

Freshly ground black pepper

3 tablespoons vegetable oil, such as sunflower or grapeseed

TOPPINGS + ADDITIONS

Cooked rice, quinoa, or grain of your choice

Fresh herbs, such as basil and mint leaves, torn

Along with chicken soup, chicken rice is one of my ultimate comfort dishes. I have good friends who have a Singaporean restaurant, and they serve the most amazing chicken rice you can get on this side of the world. Each component is simple in nature, but it has to be done just right. And when it's done right, it is just so good. This simplified version—which is much easier to make for a weeknight meal—is the perfect comfort food to make whenever you need a little cozy pick-me-up. My technique for achieving super-crispy chicken skin is something I use across all my chicken recipes. I love to serve the chicken sliced, with the addictively delicious ginger-scallion sauce over fluffy white rice with a handful of chopped herbs.

PLACE all the ingredients for the ginger-scallion sauce into a small bowl and mix to combine. Set aside while you prepare the chicken.

PAT the chicken dry with a paper towel and season with salt and pepper. This can be done a few hours ahead if you want to dry-brine the chicken for a more tender outcome and flavor.

PREHEAT the oven to 425°F. Heat the vegetable oil in a large cast-iron pan over medium-high heat for about 2 minutes. Add the chicken, skin side down, and cook for about 3 minutes undisturbed, until the skin starts to become golden brown. Flip the chicken breasts so they are skin side up and transfer to the oven. Cook for 10 to 15 minutes or until the chicken is cooked through. They are cooked through when an instant-read thermometer placed in the center reads 165°F. Remove the chicken from the oven and allow to sit for 5 minutes before slicing.

SLICE the chicken into strips and serve with the ginger-scallion sauce spooned over the top, with the rice on the side and a few torn leaves of basil and mint.

Steak with Maitake Mushroom Au Poivre

Maitake are quite possibly my favorite mushroom. And that's really saying something considering how much I adore mushrooms. When crisped, they are so meaty and tasty. The umami punch from these mushrooms added to a classic au poivre sauce, together with steak, makes this an unforgettable dish. If you want to skip the steak, you can make this vegetarian by just serving the au poivre sauce with the maitake mushrooms. And if you cannot find maitake mushrooms, shiitake mushrooms make a solid substitute.

SEASON the steak generously with salt and black pepper. Let the steak sit at room temperature for a minimum of 30 minutes or up to 2 hours.

HEAT the olive oil in a large cast-iron pan over medium heat. Add the mushrooms and cook for about 5 to 7 minutes on each side, undisturbed, until golden brown and crispy. Transfer the mushrooms to a plate while you cook the steak and sauce.

USING A MORTAR AND PESTLE, crush the peppercorns into a coarse crumb. Then, over medium-high heat, warm the vegetable oil in the same cast-iron pan you cooked the mushrooms in. When the pan is very hot, add the steak and cook undisturbed for 3 to 5 minutes, until a golden crust has formed. Flip and cook the other side until golden brown, about 3 to 5 minutes (for medium rare; if you prefer it to be more cooked through, cook for a few minutes more).

REDUCE heat to medium-low. Add the smashed garlic cloves and 1 tablespoon butter to the pan. Cook, basting steak continuously. Using an instant-read thermometer, take the steak off the pan when it reads 120°F (medium rare). Transfer steaks to a cutting board and let rest 10 minutes, while you make the sauce.

ADD the shallot, minced garlic, crushed peppercorns, and remaining 2 tablespoons butter to the skillet and cook, stirring often, until the shallot and garlic are softened but not browned, about 2 minutes. Remove from heat (to prevent a flare-up) and add the cognac to the pan. Return the pan to medium heat and cook until the cognac is mostly evaporated, about 1 to 2 minutes. Add the cream, bring to a simmer, and cook until the sauce coats a spoon, about 1 minute. Taste and add salt or additional seasoning if necessary.

SLICE the steaks and transfer to a serving plate. Pour the au poivre sauce over the top, finish with the mushrooms, and serve.

SERVES 2 TO 4

1 pound New York strip steak

Kosher salt

Freshly ground black pepper

3 tablespoons extra-virgin olive oil

8 ounces maitake mushrooms, broken into smaller pieces if large

FOR THE AU POIVRE SAUCE

1 tablespoon whole black peppercorns

2 tablespoons vegetable oil, such as sunflower or grapeseed

5 garlic cloves: 3 smashed, 2 minced, divided

3 tablespoons unsalted butter, divided

1 large shallot, finely chopped

1/3 cup cognac or sherry

1/2 cup heavy cream

Kosher salt

VEGGIE TABLES

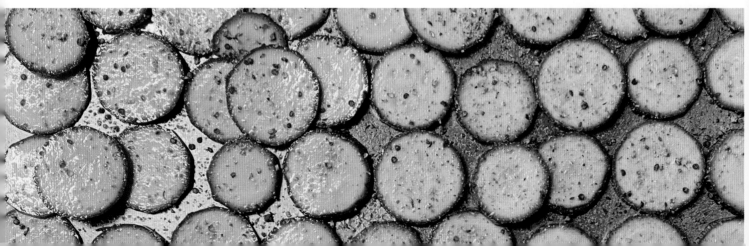

INTRO

early mornings at the farmers market.
juicy vine-ripened tomatoes in the summer,
    sliced + sprinkled with salt.
sweet roasted squash in the Fall.
Caramelized vegetables.
the change in color of produce
    as the weather gets colder.
asparagus, snap peas, + all the
    green vegetables in the spring.

Vegetables are near and dear to me. Vegetables bring out the most inspiration in my cooking, and I am constantly fascinated by their endless possibilities. At the beginning of each season, I beam with excitement with each new ingredient that appears. In the spring, the markets turn extra green thanks to the asparagus, artichokes, snap peas, and alliums. Summertime is all about abundance, color, and—of course—the juiciest tomatoes. Fall brings on the wonderful world of squashes and a shift in cooking methods to roasting and braising. And winter is about sustenance; I am always amazed at some of the heartier vegetables like kale and carrots that continue to thrive throughout the coldest months. This chapter is a bit of a love note to vegetables, showcasing some of my favorite dishes and techniques for maximizing flavor.

White Asparagus Cacio e Pepe

SERVES 2 TO 4

1 tablespoon whole black peppercorns

1 cup finely shaved Grana Padano cheese

½ cup grated Parmesan cheese

¼ cup heavy cream

2 tablespoons unsalted butter

2 tablespoons extra-virgin olive oil

1 pound white asparagus, hard ends trimmed

Kosher salt

If you've ever been to Paris during asparagus season, the white asparagus there is such a special treat. So special that you can even find it in gourmet markets preserved in jars. There is something so elegant and delicate about white asparagus, and there is something about its pure white color that gives me the urge to cover it in a creamy white sauce. This cacio e pepe version is my favorite way to indulge in these little treats. If you can't find fresh white asparagus, you can use the green instead.

HEAT a skillet over medium heat. Add the peppercorns and toast for 2 to 3 minutes. Remove and transfer to a mortar and pestle and grind until fine. Transfer the ground peppercorns to a medium mixing bowl, add the grated cheeses, and stir in the heavy cream. Whisk until the cheese has dissolved into the cream a bit. Set aside while you prepare the asparagus.

PLACE the same skillet you used to toast the peppercorns over medium heat and add the butter and olive oil. Add the asparagus and season with salt. Cook for 2 to 3 minutes, until tender and starting to turn golden brown.

ADD the cheese sauce to the asparagus and cook for about 2 minutes, until it becomes thick and creamy and coats the asparagus. Transfer to a serving plate and serve immediately.

Crisp Sautéed Zucchini with Burrata, Pesto + Roasted Tomatoes

This dish is quintessential summer to me. Zucchini and tomatoes are plentiful during this time, and I am always finding ways to make the best of their abundance. I am also always trying to find ways to prepare zucchini in ways that work with its density and high water content. Scoring and basting (more typically used for meat and seafood dishes) is my favorite method of making zucchini. It results in perfectly crisp edges with a hearty, tender, flavor-filled inside.

Pesto is another summertime staple when the basil is flourishing and begging to be used in as many dishes as possible. While this dish does not reinvent the wheel, it is the perfect example of how the best ingredients, in season, can be the ultimate simple pleasure.

PREHEAT the oven to 400°F. Place the tomatoes on a small baking sheet and drizzle with olive oil, season with salt and pepper, and toss to evenly coat. Roast the tomatoes for 30 to 35 minutes, until tender and starting to char. Remove from the oven and set aside until you're ready to assemble.

CUT each zucchini in half lengthwise, then make a crosshatch pattern across the fleshy side. Heat the olive oil in a large cast-iron pan over medium-high heat. Place the zucchini into the pan cut side down and cook undisturbed for 5 to 7 minutes, until the zucchini is starting to brown around the edges. Turn the heat down slightly to medium, flip the zucchini, and cook for about 2 minutes more, undisturbed. Then add the garlic and butter to the pan and baste the zucchini with the oil and butter for 2 to 3 minutes, until the zucchini becomes very tender and golden brown. Remove from the heat and season generously with salt and pepper.

TRANSFER the zucchini to a serving plate and scatter the roasted tomatoes over the top. Tear the burrata into pieces and scatter it evenly over the zucchini and tomatoes. Top it all with a drizzle of pesto and a few torn basil leaves, and serve.

SERVES 4

FOR THE TOMATOES

1 pint cherry tomatoes, halved

2 to 3 tablespoon extra-virgin olive oil

Kosher salt

Freshly ground black pepper

FOR THE ZUCCHINI

2 medium zucchini

¼ cup extra-virgin olive oil

3 garlic cloves, smashed

2 tablespoons unsalted butter

Kosher salt

Freshly ground black pepper

TOPPINGS + ADDITIONS

8 ounces burrata cheese

Pesto (page 192)

4 or 5 leaves fresh basil, torn

Roasted Carrots with Salsa Macha + Goat Cheese + Peanuts

SERVES 2 TO 4

1 pound carrots, scrubbed and tops trimmed

3 tablespoons extra-virgin olive oil

1 teaspoon ground cumin

Kosher salt

Freshly ground black pepper

¼ cup Salsa Macha (page 194)

¼ cup crumbled goat cheese (or feta cheese)

2 tablespoons chopped roasted peanuts

This is one of those no-brainer, minimal-effort side dishes that can be paired with so many things. As long as you have some salsa macha on hand (like I pretty much always do), this can be thrown together in no time. While I believe salsa macha can pair with anything, as well as make anything better, it really makes carrots shine because of the dance between the smoky spiciness of the macha with the sweetness of the carrots. While my version of salsa macha already has peanuts in it, I like the extra layer of crunch and nuttiness the chopped peanuts add to this dish.

PREHEAT the oven to 425°F.

PLACE the carrots on a baking sheet and toss with the olive oil and cumin, and season with salt and pepper. Roast for 20 to 30 minutes, until the carrots are fork tender and beginning to brown.

REMOVE from the oven and transfer to a serving platter. Spoon the salsa over the top, sprinkle the goat cheese and peanuts, and serve.

Shallot + Herb Mushrooms with Garlic Sourdough Croutons

Mushrooms hold a special place in my heart. In Mexico, during rainy season in the summer, the mushrooms are extremely abundant and unlike anything I've ever seen. In some areas you can find blue mushrooms, and often you can find mushrooms that are so meaty that they remind me of thick steak. I am always trying to find new and exciting ways to prepare them. For a perfect side dish, you cannot go wrong with some simple garlic-and-herb sautéed mushrooms. For this version, I added garlic croutons for a heartier panzanella vibe and because it reminds me of deconstructed mushroom toast (another favorite way for me to enjoy all the mushrooms).

PREHEAT the oven to 350°F. In a small bowl, whisk together the garlic and olive oil. Place the torn bread pieces onto a baking sheet and toss with the garlic and olive oil. Season with salt and pepper, and bake for 5 to 10 minutes (depending on how stale the bread is). You want the croutons to be golden brown and lightly crunchy, but be careful not to overcook. I like them to be a little soft in the center.

FOR THE MUSHROOMS, heat the olive oil and butter in a large cast-iron pan. Add the shallots and cook for about 1 minute, until soft. Add the mushrooms and thyme, season with salt and pepper, and stir and toss to coat with the shallot and olive oil. Cook for 5 to 7 minutes, until the mushrooms are tender and golden. When they are just about finished, add the sherry vinegar and cook for another 1 to 2 minutes, until the vinegar is evaporated and absorbed.

TRANSFER to a large serving bowl, add the garlic croutons, toss to combine, and serve.

SERVES 2 TO 4

FOR THE CROUTONS

3 garlic cloves, pressed or grated

3 tablespoons extra-virgin olive oil

2 cups torn bread, preferably 1- to 2-day-old sourdough bread, torn into 2-inch pieces

Kosher salt

Freshly ground black pepper

FOR THE MUSHROOMS

3 tablespoons extra-virgin olive oil

3 tablespoons unsalted butter

1 large shallot, sliced

1 pound mushrooms (you can use a mix; I love shiitake, maitake, oyster, and porcini—sliced or broken into smaller pieces)

1 tablespoon fresh thyme leaves (from about 3 sprigs)

Kosher salt

Freshly ground black pepper

1 tablespoon sherry vinegar

Crispy Smashed Sweet Potatoes with Yogurt + Chimichurri

MAKES 2 POTATOES

2 medium unpeeled sweet potatoes

Extra-virgin olive oil

Kosher salt

Freshly ground black pepper

TOPPINGS + ADDITIONS

⅓ cup plain whole-milk Greek yogurt

Chimichurri (page 192)

1 sliced avocado (optional)

Chopped herbs such as cilantro, parsley, or basil (optional)

This is one of my favorite vegetable dishes of all time. It is incredibly satisfying and can easily be either a side dish or a hearty vegetarian main. I personally eat this for dinner many nights when I am craving a vegetable main that is filling, delicious, and satisfying. If you are lucky enough to get your hands on the Japanese sweet potato, that to me is the best potato to use for this recipe. Regardless, any sweet potato will do. I prefer to choose a smaller size, so the crispy edges are almost equal to the tender insides. You can easily double (or triple) this dish if making it for a larger group as a side dish.

PREHEAT the oven to 450°F. Place the sweet potatoes in large pot with cold, salted water and bring to a boil. From the time it begins to boil, cook them for about 15 to 20 minutes. You want them to be fork tender but not fully cooked. They will continue to cook in the oven.

REMOVE the potatoes from the water and place on a small baking sheet. Using a spatula, press down and flatten the potato, just to crack open the skin. Generously drizzle with olive oil and season with salt and pepper. Roast for 20 to 30 minutes. You want the skins to be brown and charred around the edges. Times could vary depending on the size of the potato and your oven temperature.

TO SERVE, spread the yogurt on a serving plate and place the potatoes on top. Finish with a drizzle of the chimichurri and any additional toppings you want, and serve.

Steamed + Fried Eggplant with Ginger-Sesame Soy Sauce + Crushed Peanuts + Torn Basil

I know that eggplant can be a polarizing vegetable, but it is one that I personally love so much. I am always trying to turn eggplant haters into lovers. This is one recipe that seems to work magic on anyone who is questioning eggplant and one that will make lovers love eggplant that much more. Steaming eggplant is a foolproof way of escaping any difficulties with achieving a perfectly cooked eggplant. With the additional step of a quick sear, you then are able to achieve an amazing eggplant texture—both tender and crispy. Since eggplant is a superabsorbent vegetable, you want to make sure the sauce packs an extra flavor punch. A soy sauce laced with ginger, garlic, basil, and scallions is the perfect pairing for this eggplant preparation.

PEEL and trim the ends of the eggplants, and slice them down the middle lengthwise. Steam the eggplants flesh side down using a steamer basket, or just add them to a pot filled with about 2 inches water. Bring to a boil, cover, and steam for about 10 minutes, until the eggplants are tender. Transfer the eggplants to a cutting board, and make some slits down the inside of the middle of each piece. (I like to make a crisscross pattern.)

IN A SMALL BOWL, combine the soy sauce, vegetable oil, sesame oil, garlic, ginger, and scallion, and add a splash of water (about 1 tablespoon) to thin it out. Whisk to combine.

IN A LARGE CAST-IRON PAN, heat 1 to 2 tablespoons neutral oil over medium heat. Add the eggplants, cut side down, and cook undisturbed for 5 to 7 minutes, until the eggplant edges are crispy and golden brown. Flip and cook for another 2 to 3 minutes. Turn off the heat and pour the soy sauce over the top of the eggplants so it sizzles. Then remove the eggplants and transfer to a serving plate, spooning any remaining sauce over the top.

FINISH by topping the eggplants with a sprinkle of the sesame seeds, chopped peanuts, and torn basil.

SERVES 2 TO 4

2 (6- to 8-ounce) eggplants, preferably Japanese

2 to 3 tablespoons vegetable oil, such as sunflower or grapeseed

FOR THE SAUCE

3 tablespoons soy sauce or tamari

1 tablespoon vegetable oil, such as sunflower or grapeseed

1 teaspoon sesame oil

2 garlic cloves, grated

1 ($\frac{1}{2}$-inch) piece of fresh ginger, peeled and grated

1 scallion, thinly sliced

TOPPINGS + ADDITIONS

1 tablespoon toasted sesame seeds

1 tablespoon roasted, unsalted, finely chopped peanuts

3 or 4 fresh basil leaves, torn

Roasted Fennel with Harissa Quinoa
+ Fennel Frond Gremolata

SERVES 2 TO 4

FOR THE QUINOA

½ cup quinoa, rinsed

1 cup chicken broth or water

1 tablespoon harissa paste

FOR THE FENNEL

1 fennel bulb

2 to 3 tablespoons extra-virgin olive oil

Kosher salt

Freshly ground black pepper

FOR THE FENNEL FROND GREMOLATA

Reserved fennel fronds

Zest from 1 lemon

1 garlic clove, grated or pressed

Kosher salt

When roasted and caramelized, fennel develops into something really special—special enough to be the main event. This surprising star side dish has quinoa to add a bit of oomph and makes for a great delivery vehicle for the fennel. And if you don't have harissa handy, or prefer something without spice, you could easily swap in a pesto or another sauce or dressing of your choice. Most importantly, you cannot ignore the fennel fronds. They are the added bonus of the vegetable. I love to toss them with some garlic and lemon zest to make a gremolata which makes this whole dish sing.

PLACE the quinoa and broth or water into a small saucepan over high heat and bring to a boil. Season with salt to taste; if using a chicken broth that is salty, you might not need to add salt at all. Once it's boiling, reduce to a simmer, cover, and cook for 15 minutes, until the quinoa is fully cooked. Remove from heat, stir in the harissa paste, and set aside.

PREHEAT the oven to 350°F.

PREPARE the fennel by slicing the bulb away from the longer green stems, then slice the bulb in half. Remove the fennel fronds and reserve them for the gremolata. Chop the remaining longer green parts into 1-inch chunks.

PLACE the fennel halves and chopped pieces onto a small baking sheet, drizzle with olive oil, and season with salt and pepper. Roast for 20 to 30 minutes, until tender and golden brown around the edges.

WHILE THE FENNEL IS ROASTING, make the gremolata. In a small mixing bowl, combine the fennel fronds, lemon zest, and garlic. Season with a pinch of salt, and stir.

PLACE the harissa quinoa onto a serving platter. Lay the fennel halves on top and scatter the smaller chopped pieces all around. Finish by sprinkling the gremolata over the top, and serve.

Esquites with Chili + Lime + Cotija Cheese

Esquites is a super-popular and very delicious street food in Mexico. Esquites refers to corn kernels, and in Mexico they are typically served tossed together with a generous helping of mayo, a sprinkle of chili powder, and some Cotija cheese (a crumbly cheese from Mexico that is mild but adds a salty punch). While this recipe uses all of those standard ingredients found in the Mexican street food, I also added some freshly chopped chives, cilantro, minced jalapeño, and garlic to the mix to give it freshness that makes for a perfect side dish, especially in summertime. If you cannot find Cotija cheese, feta or crumbled goat cheese would make an excellent substitution.

HEAT the oil in a large cast-iron pan over medium heat. Add the corn kernels, season with salt and pepper, and sauté for 3 to 5 minutes until the kernels are tender. Remove from the heat.

IN A LARGE MIXING BOWL, stir the mayonnaise, lime juice, chives, garlic, jalapeño, and chili powder, and season with salt and pepper. Add the corn to the mixture and stir to combine. Toss in the cilantro and Cotija cheese, stir again to incorporate, and serve.

SERVES 4

2 tablespoons extra-virgin olive oil

3 ears of corn, kernels removed (about 3 cups)

Kosher salt

Freshly ground black pepper

¼ cup mayonnaise

Juice from 1 lime

¼ cup chives, minced

1 garlic clove, grated or pressed

1 jalapeño, seeded and finely minced

½ teaspoon chili powder or smoked paprika

1 handful fresh cilantro, chopped

½ cup Cotija cheese, or crumbled feta or goat cheese

Charred Broccoli with
Feta + Almonds + Lemon

SERVES 2 TO 4

2 to 3 tablespoons extra-virgin olive oil

1 broccoli head, chopped into florets

Kosher salt

¼ cup slivered almonds

Juice and zest from ½ lemon

¼ cup feta cheese, crumbled

Freshly ground black pepper

For my very first job out of college and not in a restaurant, I worked as a production assistant for a photographer in his studio space. It required many hours alone at the computer and eating at my desk almost every day. On the days that my boss would come to the office, he would make me lunch. He was mostly vegetarian, and he was obsessed with broccoli. More often than not, he would make us this crispy broccoli dish that he would top with almonds (lightly toasted in a toaster oven), along with a sprinkling of feta cheese, and a squeeze of lemon juice. It was surprisingly tasty and a dish I still crave all these years later.

CUT the broccoli florets in half—for a flat surface—then toss them with the olive oil and season with salt. Heat a large cast-iron pan over medium-high heat. Add the broccoli to the pan, flat side down to get maximum char, and cook undisturbed for about 2 minutes, until the broccoli starts to brown and become tender. Toss and flip the florets and cook on the other side for about 2 minutes more, until they are at the tenderness you desire.

REMOVE the pan from the heat, transfer the broccoli to a serving plate, and wipe the pan clean with a towel. Return the pan to medium heat, add a drizzle of olive oil and the almonds. Cook for 2 to 3 minutes, until the almond slivers are light brown and lightly toasted.

SPRINKLE the almonds over the broccoli. Add the lemon juice, lemon zest, and feta cheese over the top, and some black pepper, and serve.

SWEETS

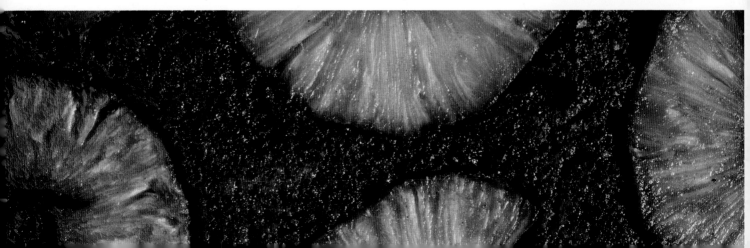

INTRO

the smell of freshly baked cookies
filling your home.

sweetened whipped crème fraiche or mascarpone.

warm cake, cold ice cream.

pie in the summertime.

one dessert, two spoons.

crunchy, creamy, cold + warm in one bite.

salty sweets.

While I don't consider myself a "dessert person," I get great joy from creating desserts, often using my nostalgic tastes and memories to guide the recipes. I like desserts that are simple, foolproof, sometimes messy, and they often have some sort of memory attached to them. My mom had an amazing repertoire of simple desserts—many that I still make to this day. I have included some of these recipes with added twists like savory elements or the addition of an unexpected texture or flavor to take it to the next level.

Olive Oil Panna Cotta with Sweet Balsamic Drizzle

SERVES 6

2½ teaspoons powdered gelatin (1 packet)

1 cup whole milk, cold

1 tablespoon fresh lemon juice

½ cup granulated sugar

½ teaspoon vanilla extract

Pinch of kosher salt

2 cups heavy cream

Extra-virgin olive oil

FOR THE SWEET BALSAMIC DRIZZLE

1 cup balsamic vinegar

3 tablespoons granulated sugar

I cannot find enough ways to incorporate olive oil into sweets. This recipe—the perfect intersection of sweet, savory, and tangy—really highlights just how magical a zesty olive oil can be in a dessert. The balsamic glaze that gets cooked down so that it is equal parts sweet and acidic is the perfect punchy accompaniment. This panna cotta is also a good base for getting creative with any other toppings, such as a sweet conserve or crunch element.

POUR the gelatin, cold milk, and lemon juice into a small saucepan and allow it to sit for 5 minutes to bloom. Turn the heat on low and stir to dissolve the gelatin, about 3 to 5 minutes.

REMOVE from heat and add the sugar, vanilla, and salt. Stir until the sugar is dissolved. Strain the mixture into a bowl to get rid of any leftover gelatin bits, then add the heavy cream and stir to combine.

PREPARE 6 ramekins or small bowls by drizzling a tiny amount of olive oil into the bottom of each ramekin and brushing it up the sides.

DISTRIBUTE the panna cotta evenly among the ramekins. Cover with plastic wrap and refrigerate for at least 3 hours. You can also make this a couple of days in advance and store in the fridge until you're ready to serve.

TO MAKE THE BALSAMIC DRIZZLE, add the balsamic vinegar and sugar to a small saucepan. Bring to a simmer over medium heat, and then reduce to low and cook for about 15 minutes while stirring often, to reduce the sauce and concentrate the sugars. When the mixture has a syrup-like texture, remove from heat and allow to cool slightly.

DRIZZLE the balsamic glaze and a little extra olive oil over the top of each panna cotta and serve.

Date Cake with No-Churn Tahini Ice Cream + Bourbon-Soaked Dates

I have always been in love with the sticky, addictive texture of date cake. Since tahini ice cream is not something you commonly find, I knew I had to make my own simplified version, so I turned to the easy no-churn method that uses condensed milk to create the ice-cream texture without all the work. Of course, you could skip the ice cream (making) part and use something store-bought instead. A scoop of vanilla and a drizzle of tahini would be mighty fine as well, especially when topped with the bourbon-soaked dates.

START by making the ice cream (5 hours to 1 day ahead). Using a stand or hand mixer, whip the heavy cream until fluffy and stiff peaks have formed, about 5 to 7 minutes. In an 8 x 8 square cake pan or 9 x 5 loaf pan, whisk together the condensed milk, tahini, and vanilla. Pour the whipped cream into the pan and, using a rubber spatula, gently fold the cream into the tahini mixture until it's fully combined. Freeze for 5 hours. (Plan to remove from the freezer 10 minutes before serving.)

TO MAKE THE CAKE, preheat the oven to 350°F. Grease a 9 x 13 baking dish with butter or olive oil.

PLACE one-third of the dates (½ pound) into a small bowl and pour the bourbon over the top. Set aside to soak while you make the cake.

PLACE 2½ cups water in a small pot, bring to a boil, and then remove from the heat. Add the remaining 1 pound of dates and the baking soda. Let them sit for about 10 minutes until the dates have broken down a bit. Mash them with a fork to break them down a bit more.

PLACE the sugar, eggs, and vanilla extract in the bowl of a stand mixer with the whisk attachment; you can also use a large bowl and a hand mixer. Mix on medium speed until the sugar is incorporated and the mixture is thick and can coat the back of a spoon, about 5 minutes. Add in the flour and baking powder and beat on low until just incorporated, about 1 minute. Pour the batter into the greased baking dish and bake for 35 to 40 minutes, until a cake tester poked into the center comes out clean.

TO SERVE, cut the cake into squares and place onto individual serving plates. Serve each piece with a scoop of the ice cream and a bourbon-soaked date.

MAKES 1 (9- X 13-INCH) CAKE, 10 TO 12 SLICES

FOR THE TAHINI ICE CREAM

2 cups heavy cream

1 (14-ounce) can sweetened condensed milk

½ cup tahini

2 vanilla beans, scraped (or 2 tablespoons vanilla bean paste)

FOR THE DATE CAKE

1 tablespoon unsalted butter or extra-virgin olive oil, for greasing the pan

1½ pounds medjool dates, pitted; divided

½ cup bourbon, whiskey, or rum

2½ cups water

1 tablespoon baking soda

1½ cups granulated sugar

2 large eggs

1 tablespoon vanilla extract

2½ cups all-purpose flour

2 teaspoons baking powder

Salty Mezcal Pineapple Upside-Down Cake

MAKES 1 (9-INCH) ROUND CAKE, ABOUT 12 SLICES

FOR THE TOPPING

1 small pineapple, peeled, cored, and sliced into ⅛-inch-thick rounds and then sliced in half (I find you can get more pineapple coverage with the half-moon shape)

½ to 1 cup mezcal

½ cup (1 stick) unsalted butter

½ cup panela or light brown sugar, packed

1 teaspoon flaky sea salt

FOR THE CAKE

1 cup all-purpose flour

¾ cup granulated sugar

½ teaspoon kosher salt

½ teaspoon baking soda

2 large eggs, lightly beaten

½ cup unsweetened coconut milk

½ cup (1 stick) unsalted butter, melted

1 tablespoon fresh lime juice

1 teaspoon vanilla extract

This cake is one of my prized creations. During the time when we had a lot of extra time to bake, and maybe even a little extra booze around to pass the time, I knew I needed to make a boozy cake. One of my favorite, magical, nostalgic desserts has to be pineapple upside-down cake. While mezcal is my personal favorite liquor here, you can also make this cake using tequila or rum (both would be delicious), or you can leave out the booze all together—especially if you are serving this to kids (the pineapple ends up being quite boozy; be warned). You will likely have a little leftover pineapple and the booze it was marinating in. You will want to save that, covered in the fridge, for cocktails. (Or eat and drink it yourself while your cake is baking . . . no judgments here whatsoever.) This cake would be extra special served with some ice cream or whole-milk Greek yogurt.

PREHEAT the oven to 350°F.

TO MAKE THE TOPPING, place the sliced pineapple on a small baking sheet and pour the mezcal over top. You might need a little more than ½ cup depending on your pan size. Marinate the pineapple for 2 to 3 hours or up to overnight. This step is optional, but if you don't have the time or desire a boozy cake you can start with the next step.

MELT the butter in a 9-inch cast-iron pan or a regular skillet over medium heat. Add the panela or brown sugar, and cook while stirring constantly until the sugar has dissolved, about 5 minutes. Remove from heat, sprinkle the salt evenly over the caramel topping, and add the pineapple, arranging the slices in whatever design you like. Set aside while you prepare the batter.

IN A LARGE MIXING BOWL, add the flour, sugar, salt, and baking soda, and stir to combine. Make a well in the center of the flour mixture and add the eggs, coconut milk, melted butter, lime juice, and vanilla. Stir to combine within the well, then fold into the flour mixture until you form a smooth batter. Pour the batter into the skillet over the pineapple and smooth the top. Bake for 30 to 40 minutes, until a cake tester comes out clean. I'd encourage you to bake a little longer—maybe 5 or so minutes past done—if you want crispy edges. When the cake is done, allow to rest for at least 10 minutes, then using a plate that is slightly larger than the skillet, hold the plate up against the skillet and carefully flip the cake onto the plate. You can then slice and enjoy warm. This cake will last a couple days, covered, at room temperature.

Marinated Strawberries with Meringue + Whipped Crème Fraîche

Meringue is one of my favorite desserts to make for events or dinner parties because it can be made in advance and it's always a crowd pleaser—the flavor isn't too sweet and the texture pairs with and enhances so many things. This is one of my favorite ways to serve it, and in some cases this is very similar to the dessert called Eton mess. In my version, I like to make it very messy and pair it with a not-too-sweet crème fraîche whip and strawberries that have been marinating in a boozy liquid. Of course, you could substitute strawberries for any other fruit that is in season. Also, if you want to leave out the booze, balsamic vinegar would be a delicious and intriguing substitute.

IN A MEDIUM BOWL, add the lime juice and zest, sugar, rum, and mint and whisk to combine. Add the strawberries and toss to combine. Allow to marinate while you prepare the meringue and whip.

PREHEAT the oven to 350°F. Line a large baking sheet with parchment paper. Using a stand mixer with the whisk attachment, whisk the egg whites until they form stiff peaks. Add the vanilla, and add in the sugar 1 tablespoon at a time until the mixture is thick and glossy.

PLACE dollops of the meringue onto the baking sheet. Reduce the oven temperature to 200°F right before placing the meringues into the oven. Bake for about 1 hour (sometimes up to 1 hour and 30 minutes, depending on your oven), until the meringues are completely hard. Remove and allow to cool.

CLEAN the bowl and whisk of the stand mixer you used to make the meringue, and using the same whisk attachment, add the crème fraîche, heavy cream, and sugar and whisk on high until thick and creamy, about 2 minutes.

TO ASSEMBLE, break apart the meringues in a messy fashion onto a large serving platter. Then scatter dollops of the whipped crème fraîche evenly around the meringue. Lastly, add the strawberries and the juices over the top. Finish with a scattering of the basil and mint.

SERVES 10 TO 12

FOR THE STRAWBERRIES

Zest and juice from 1 lime

2 tablespoons granulated sugar

2 tablespoons dark rum

5 to 7 fresh mint leaves, sliced into thin ribbons

2 cups strawberries, hulled and halved

FOR THE MERINGUE

2 large egg whites

1 teaspoon vanilla extract

½ cup (superfine) caster sugar

FOR THE WHIPPED CRÈME FRAÎCHE

¼ cup crème fraîche

¼ cup heavy cream

2 teaspoons granulated sugar

TOPPINGS + ADDITIONS

Fresh basil leaves, torn

Fresh mint leaves, torn

Sheet-Pan Olive Oil Chocolate Cake
with Hibiscus Buttercream

MAKES 1 (9- X 13-INCH) CAKE, 12 TO 15 SLICES

FOR THE CAKE

1⅓ cups extra-virgin olive oil, plus more for greasing the pan

2 cups granulated sugar

6 large eggs

⅔ cup cocoa powder

1 cup fresh orange juice

1 tablespoon vanilla extract

3 cups almond flour

1 teaspoon baking soda

½ teaspoon kosher salt

FOR THE BUTTERCREAM

4 cups powdered sugar

1½ cups unsalted butter, room temperature

¼ cup sour cream or crème fraîche

2 to 4 tablespoons hibiscus flower juice (see note above)

In my first cookbook, one of the most popular recipes was a flourless chocolate cake. I would often double the recipe because people could just never get enough of that cake and would often eat 2 to 3 pieces in one sitting. It's light, moist, and addictively delicious. Since then, I have made a few other tweaks, with the addition of a sour cream buttercream that gets a hint of pink from soaked hibiscus flower (a plentiful ingredient here in Mexico). If you don't care for the pink color, you can simply omit the hibiscus. You could even make a chocolate-frosting version by adding about 6 ounces of melted chocolate to the mix.

Note: *To make the hibiscus flower juice, combine 1 cup hibiscus flowers and 4 to 5 cups water to a pot and simmer on medium-low heat for 10 to 15 minutes. You can reserve the extra juice and drink it as tea, or add a bit of sugar to the water and drink it chilled. You can also reserve the flowers and add them as a topping for decoration.*

PREHEAT the oven to 350°F. Grease a 9 x 13 cake pan with a bit of olive oil and line the bottom with parchment paper.

PUT the sugar, eggs, and 1⅓ cups olive oil in the bowl of a stand mixer with the whisk attachment and whisk on high until a thick cream has formed, enough to coat the back of a spoon. Reduce the speed to medium-low and add in the cocoa powder, orange juice, and vanilla and whisk for about a minute to combine. Then slowly add in the almond flour, baking soda, and salt while the mixer is running. Allow to mix for another minute to make sure the ingredients are fully combined.

POUR the batter into the cake pan and bake for 40 to 45 minutes, until a cake tester poked in the center comes out clean.

WHILE THE CAKE IS BAKING, prepare the buttercream. Clean out the bowl used for the stand mixer and change to a paddle attachment. Sift the powdered sugar into the bowl, to make sure there is no clumping of the sugar. Add in the softened butter and sour cream and beat on medium-high speed until combined and smooth, about 1 minute. Then add in the hibiscus flower juice and beat for another minute to incorporate.

ALLOW the cake to cool to room temperature before frosting. When you're ready to frost, add the frosting to the center of the cake and, using a rubber spatula, smooth the frosting in an even layer over the cake. Place the frosted cake in the fridge for 15 to 20 minutes before serving so that the slices come out clean. Cut the cake into square slices, and serve.

Blueberry Surprise with Shortbread Crumble + Mascarpone Whip

This dessert is a riff on a dessert my mom used to make all the time, especially in the peak of summer when the blueberries were plump and plentiful. However, this dessert is also super adaptable for all seasons and fruits. Her version was one of those semi-homemade kinds that had some sort of store-bought cookie crumbled as the base, topped with gently simmered blueberries and heaps of whipped cream (maybe even sometimes a whole container of Cool Whip). The biggest surprise in this version is not actually the blueberries—it's that as you scoop down to the bottom, you get a delicious crunchy treat from the homemade shortbread, making this total textural dream come true.

PREHEAT the oven to 350°F. Line a large baking sheet with parchment paper.

PLACE the softened butter into the bowl of a stand mixer with the whisk attachment. Whip the butter on high speed for 2 to 3 minutes, until very soft. Reduce the speed, add in the sugar, and whip until combined. Add the flour a ¼ cup at a time, then the salt, and mix until combined and the dough is crumbly and slightly wet. Be sure to push down the sides and help the dough along during this process.

ADD the dough to the baking sheet, and press to flatten a bit. You're going to be crumbling this at the bottom of the dessert so there is no need to be perfect here. You just want a flat even surface for even baking.

BAKE for 25 to 30 minutes, until golden brown. Remove from the oven to cool. Once cooled, crumble into the bottom of a baking dish, bowl, or whatever vessel you want to use.

PLACE the blueberries, lime juice, cornstarch, sugar, and salt into a large saucepan over medium heat. Cook, while occasionally stirring, for 10 minutes, until the berries are tender but still holding their shape. Pour the cooked blueberries over the shortbread and then place it in the fridge to cool for at least 20 minutes while you make the mascarpone whip.

IN THE SAME STAND MIXER with whisk attachment, add the mascarpone, heavy cream, powdered sugar, vanilla, and salt, and whip on high until the cream is stiff but fluffy, about 1 minute. Once the blueberries have cooled a bit, add the whipped mascarpone on top.

YOU CAN SERVE IMMEDIATELY, but I like to serve it when the whole dish has cooled in the fridge a bit. This can be made 1 to 2 days in advance.

SERVES 10 TO 12

FOR THE SHORTBREAD
½ cup (1 stick) unsalted butter, softened

½ cup granulated sugar

1½ cups all-purpose flour

½ teaspoon kosher salt

FOR THE BLUEBERRIES
1 pound fresh blueberries, or any other kind of berry or fruit

Juice from ½ lime

2 tablespoons cornstarch

¼ cup granulated sugar

¼ teaspoon kosher salt

FOR THE MASCARPONE WHIP
1 cup mascarpone

1 cup heavy cream

1 tablespoon powdered sugar

1 teaspoon vanilla extract

¼ teaspoon kosher salt

Pie de Limón
(Mexican Lime Pie)

MAKES 8 TO 10 SLICES

½ cup fresh lime juice (from about 5 limes)

12 ounces unsweetened, canned coconut milk (full-fat)

12 ounces sweetened condensed milk

1 teaspoon vanilla extract

½ teaspoon kosher salt

24 to 36 Maria cookies or ladyfingers

TOPPINGS + ADDITIONS

Zest from 1 lime

3 fresh mint leaves, thinly sliced

Plain whole-milk Greek yogurt or sour cream

Pie de limón is a super nostalgic dessert in Mexico. Many of my friends here have told me that the taste reminds them of their childhood. I love this dessert because it is so easy to make but also because it feels like a hybrid of two of my favorite desserts of all time: key lime pie and tiramisu. The cream base used to make this is very similar in ingredients to what is used in key lime pie filling, and the cookie base is similar to how a tiramisu is layered. If you cannot find the traditional Mexican cookie (Maria cookies) to make this, you could also use the ladyfingers used for tiramisu. My recipe strays just slightly from the traditional recipe by substituting coconut milk for evaporated milk, imparting a lovely coconut flavor.

COMBINE the lime juice, coconut milk, sweetened condensed milk, vanilla, and salt in a blender. Blend until smooth and creamy.

IN AN 8- X 8-INCH BAKING DISH, pour a little bit of the cream on the bottom, and add a layer of cookies on top. Cover the cookies with more cream, then add another layer of cookies on top of that. Do this until you have 3 to 4 layers of cookies, using all of the cream to cover the cookies completely so that they absorb the sweet liquid. Smooth the top, cover with plastic wrap, and refrigerate for a minimum of 2 hours, but even better for 5 hours or overnight.

WHEN the pie has solidified, it is ready to serve. Slice into individual servings and top with lime zest, the sliced mint leaves, and a spoonful of yogurt or sour cream.

Double Chocolate Miso + Brown Butter Cookies

I am a big fan of adding miso to sweets. It adds this secret kind of umami punch that really amplifies the richness in the best way. The first time I had miso in a cookie, it blew my mind. It was a basic chocolate chip cookie but the miso just gave it something a little extra. With this recipe, I decided to take it to another level with the addition of brown butter and double chocolate—cocoa powder and chocolate chunks.

PREHEAT the oven to 375°F. Line a large baking sheet with parchment paper.

IN A LARGE BOWL, mix together the flour, sugars, cocoa powder, baking soda, and salt. Make a well in the center of the flour and add in the egg. Stir until it's fully incorporated. Set aside while you prepare the miso chocolate.

HEAT a frying pan over medium heat. Melt the butter in the pan and cook, swirling often, while the butter is bubbling. Do this until the butter becomes brown and smells nutty, about 3 to 4 minutes. Add the miso, dark chocolate (6 ounces), and vanilla and stir constantly using a silicone spatula, until the ingredients are completely melted and combined. Pour the mixture into the bowl with the flour and sugar, and stir to incorporate.

SCOOP about 2 tablespoons dough and form it into a ball. Place it onto a baking sheet, and repeat with the remaining dough, spacing the dough balls about 2 inches apart to allow for the cookies to spread when cooking. Place a chunk of chocolate (from the 1 ounce reserved) into the center of each dough ball and sprinkle with flaky sea salt. Bake for 15 minutes, until the edges look set and the cookies are slightly firm to the touch. They will be on the softer side but will harden a bit as they cool. Remove from the oven and allow to cool on the baking sheet. These cookies will keep for about a week in an airtight container at room temperature.

MAKES 12 TO 14 COOKIES

1½ cups all-purpose flour

½ cup light brown sugar

½ cup granulated sugar

¼ cup cocoa powder

1 teaspoon baking soda

¼ teaspoon of kosher salt

1 large egg, lightly beaten

½ cup (1 stick) unsalted butter

¼ cup red miso

7 ounces dark chocolate (70 percent), divided (1 ounce reserved and roughly chopped)

1 teaspoon vanilla extract

1 teaspoon flaky salt, for topping

ESSENTIAL SAUCES

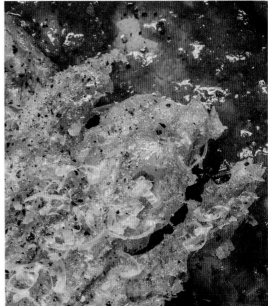

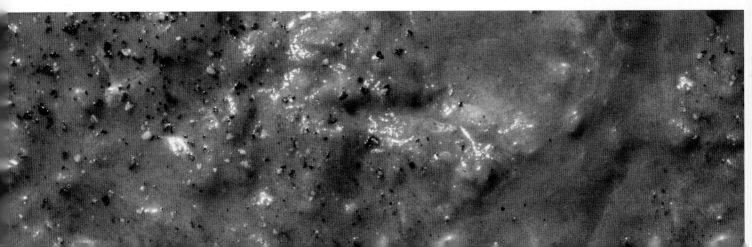

INTRO

dipping a french fry into aioli.
garlicky pesto over fresh pasta.
emulsification.
steak + chimichurri.
baguette + aioli.
toasted bread + flavored butter.

I am the biggest fan of condiments, especially because their main role is to enhance any overall meal. If you open my fridge, you will always find a collection of homemade sauces and condiments—I have been called the "queen of condiments," which is the highest compliment in my eyes. While I have made and experimented with hundreds of sauces over the years, this chapter highlights a select few of my most-satisfying, most-craved sauces and condiments. I also provide a template for each so that you can feel free to experiment and build your own sauces, as you wish.

Ode to Aioli

Aioli is one of the greatest gifts of all condiments. Creamy, tangy, and pairs with just about anything: a dipping sauce for crispy potatoes, French fries, or vegetables; slathering it onto hamburgers; drizzling over tacos—the list can go on and on. This is probably one of my most-made condiments, and the variations are endless. Below is my basic recipe. You can use this as a template and add just about any herbs, spices, chilies, or other flavors, such as anchovies or mustard.

A couple of notes about making aioli: It's important that your egg is room temperature. You will have trouble emulsifying if you use a cold egg. I also prefer to use a neutral oil because olive oil can have a strong flavor. If you prefer to make it with olive oil, just be aware of the flavor it will impart. Lastly, while making aioli by hand is always acceptable, I prefer the ease of a food processor.

GARLIC AIOLI

MAKES 1 CUP

1 garlic clove

2 teaspoons kosher salt

Freshly ground black pepper

1 tablespoon fresh lemon juice

1 large egg, room temperature

3/4 to 1 cup vegetable oil, such as sunflower, grapeseed, or canola

PLACE the garlic into a mortar and pestle with the salt and some black pepper. Grind until the mixture is a smooth paste. Squeeze the lemon juice into the mortar and stir and mash to combine with the garlic paste. Transfer the paste to the bowl of a food processor and add the egg. Give it a few pulses to combine, and then while it's running continuously, drizzle in the oil in a slow stream until you have a smooth, thick, and creamy texture. Taste and adjust any seasoning you feel is necessary. Serve immediately or store for 1 to 2 weeks in an airtight container in the fridge.

VARIATIONS

Just add these to the food processor along with the other ingredients before adding the oil:

Anchovy + chive (1 to 2 anchovy filets + 1 tablespoon minced chives)

Dill + mustard (2 teaspoons mustard + 1 tablespoon fresh dill)

Cilantro + lime + jalapeño (1 tablespoon chopped cilantro + change out the lemon for lime + 1 jalapeño, seeded and minced)

Roasted garlic + saffron (3 to 4 roasted garlic cloves + pinch of saffron)

Chipotle (1 large chipotle in adobo)

Chive or ramp (1/4 cup minced chives or ramps)

For the Love of Flavored Butter

Butter, to me, is happiness. Is there any greater simple joy than smearing some softened salted butter over a slice of crusty bread? It is my favorite cooking fat. Just like aioli, flavored butters have a top place in my condiment arsenal. They are great to have around for a quick and flavorful dinner, but they are also helpful in creating something to impress. Outside of smearing on some fresh bread, I particularly like to use compound butters for basting meat, fish, or vegetables in a cast-iron pan. Or you can go the sweet route and melt it over pancakes, crepes, or other desserts or pastries. Making compound butter ahead of time or ensuring you have some extra will keep you prepared for a quick and delicious meal.

IN A MIXING BOWL, fold in your flavorings of choice or use a food processor to ensure a cohesive mixture and more whipped texture. To store, use plastic wrap or parchment paper to roll it into a log, then wrap it and store in the fridge for up to 2 weeks or transfer to the freezer to store for up to 6 months.

MAKES 8 TABLESPOONS (1 STICK) BUTTER

8 tablespoons (1 stick) butter, preferably salted, softened

Flavorings of choice

SOME FAVORITE FLAVOR COMBINATIONS

Tomato confit + roasted garlic ($\frac{1}{4}$ cup tomato confit (page 197) + 2 to 3 roasted garlic cloves)

Wild garlic + lemon zest (3 to 4 pieces wild garlic or ramps, white and green parts, minced + zest of 1 lemon)

Anchovy + parsley + shallot (2 to 3 anchovy filets + 2 tablespoons flat-leaf parsley, finely chopped + 1 large shallot, minced)

Chili crisp (3 tablespoons chili crisp)

Bacon + scallion (4 to 5 pieces crispy bacon, finely chopped + 2 scallions, thinly sliced)

Pesto ($\frac{1}{4}$ cup Pesto, page 192)

Salted maple ($\frac{1}{4}$ cup pure maple syrup + pinch of ground cinnamon + 2 teaspoons flaky sea salt)

Lemon sugar (1 tablespoon granulated sugar + zest of 1 lemon)

SALSA MACHA
(page 194)

CHIMICHURRI
(page 192)

**LEMON SUGAR, CHIVE,
AND TOMATO CONFIT
FLAVORED BUTTERS**
(page 189)

**CLASSIC SHALLOT
SHERRY VINAIGRETTE**
(page 196)

TOMATO CONFIT
(page 197)

GARLIC AIOLI
(page 188)

Pesto + Chimichurri

These garlic-forward condiments are forever classic and beloved accompaniments to so many meals. Pasta, steak, veggies, fish—there is nothing that these two powerhouse sauces cannot make better. There are also many varieties that you can try, so I am sharing the base recipes and a few of my favorite additions or ways to play around with flavor.

CHIMICHURRI

MAKES APPROXIMATELY 1 CUP

⅓ cup red, white, or yellow onion, or even scallion or green onion

3 to 4 garlic cloves

1 green chili, seeded

2 cups flat-leaf parsley or cilantro or a combination of both

½ cup extra-virgin olive oil

2 to 3 tablespoons red wine, white wine, or sherry vinegar

Kosher salt

Freshly ground black pepper

BECAUSE I LIKE CHIMICHURRI TO HAVE LOTS OF TEXTURE, I mince the onion, garlic, and chili together on a cutting board, then add the herbs, chopping to incorporate. Transfer to a bowl before covering with the olive oil and vinegar, and season to taste with salt and pepper.

ADDITIONS

1 whole avocado, chopped

½ cup yogurt

PESTO

MAKES APPROXIMATELY 1 CUP

⅓ cup of nuts or seeds, preferably toasted

1 to 3 garlic cloves

2 cups fresh herbs or leafy greens (such as basil, flat-leaf parsley, spinach, or kale)

½ cup cheese (typically a grated salty hard cheese, such as Parmesan, but I have also used a soft cheese, such as ricotta, for a creamier outcome)

About 1 cup extra-virgin olive oil

Squeeze of lemon juice (optional, if you want some acidity)

Kosher salt, to taste

Freshly ground black pepper, to taste

IN A BLENDER OR FOOD PROCESSOR, blend the ingredients while drizzling in the olive oil.

ADDITIONS

Olives

Capers

Anchovies

Salsa Macha

MAKES ABOUT 3 CUPS

10 pasilla chilies

20 morita chilies

1 cup plus ¼ cup vegetable oil, such as canola, sunflower, or grapeseed, divided

2 cups diced white onion

10 garlic cloves, minced

Kosher salt

⅓ cup white sesame seeds

⅓ cup peanuts, roughly chopped

1 tablespoon natural peanut butter

2 teaspoons tamari

Salsa macha is the queen of all salsas. It is such a special sauce that it made me fall deeply in love with Mexico and its cuisine. When first discovering salsa macha, I was excited and intrigued by the intertwining dance between the spicy, dried red chilies and the richness and crunch of the nuts. As I have learned from years of making and discussing salsa macha, there is not just one traditional way of making it. Throughout Mexico you will find endless variations, and it's not only accepted but also encouraged to play around and experiment with different variations of chilies, nuts, and seeds as well as add-ins such as garlic, onion, and even (though less traditional) soy sauce or sesame oil.

I started working on variations of this recipe when I first arrived in Mexico. I consulted one of my dear friends, who is Mexican and is currently the head chef at one of the best restaurants in the world. Pablo taught me a lot about the world of Mexican cuisine, and we share the same passion for salsa macha and its endless possibilities. This version is my personal favorite base to play around with. It is a little more labor intensive than some other salsa macha recipes because I like to take some time to caramelize the garlic and onion and deseed all the chilies. But the effort is well worth it for the intense flavor. The secret special ingredient in my personal recipe: peanut butter, which gives it that "why is this so good" hint of flavor.

Feel free to experiment with your own version by using different dried red chilies, nuts, seeds, or other flavor enhancers.

TOAST the chilis in a comal, cast-iron pan, or frying pan over medium heat, just until they puff, about 2 minutes. Remove from heat, discard the stems and all or most of the seeds (depending on how spicy you want it to be).

HEAT ¼ cup neutral oil in a shallow pot over medium heat, and add the onions, garlic, and a hearty 2 pinches of salt. Cook for 15 to 20 minutes, until the onions have cooked down a bit and are starting to caramelize and turn golden brown. Be sure to adjust the heat as needed so they don't cook too fast or burn. Add the sesame seeds, peanuts, and another pinch of salt. Cook for 2 to 4 minutes, until the nuts and seeds are lightly toasted. Remove from heat and divide the mixture in half: one half is added to the chilies and blended; the other half is reserved for textural contrast in the end.

USING THE SAME POT that you cooked the onions in (no need to clean, as long as you removed all the onion-garlic bits), heat the remaining 1 cup oil over medium heat. Add the chilies and cook for about 2 minutes, until they become a bright, deep red. As they are changing color, that is when you want to add half of the onion-garlic-nut-seed mixture. Lower the heat slightly and cook for another 2 minutes.

REMOVE from the heat and carefully pour the mixture into a blender, add the peanut butter and tamari, and blend on high for about 2 minutes, until the salsa is super smooth. Feel free to add more oil if it's too thick or until you achieve the texture you desire. Taste for seasoning and adjust if necessary. Pour the salsa into a medium bowl, then add the remaining half of the onion-garlic-nut-seed mixture and stir. Transfer to a large jar or a couple of small jars. It will last a couple of months in an airtight jar in the fridge.

My Go-To Dressing + Marinade

I think it is super important as a home cook to have dressings or marinades that are either already prepared and ready to go or that you can make easily for when you want to whip up a salad for lunch or a quick, healthy dinner. For dressings, you can never ever go wrong with a basic vinaigrette that has classic ingredients such as Dijon mustard and a punchy vinegar. Similar with a marinade. I also would like to think that these two acid-forward recipes could easily work interchangeably.

CLASSIC SHALLOT SHERRY VINAIGRETTE

MAKES ABOUT ½ CUP

2 tablespoons shallots, finely minced

2 tablespoons sherry vinegar

2 teaspoons Dijon mustard

½ teaspoon kosher salt

Freshly ground black pepper, to taste

⅓ cup extra-virgin olive oil

With this recipe, you could easily change around some of the ingredients, using the same proportions, to play with different flavors. I like sherry vinegar for its tangy sweetness, but you could also try a white wine, red wine, apple cider, or champagne vinegar. Same with switching up the mustard for different varieties. Also, the addition of dried or fresh herbs would play well here.

PLACE the shallot, vinegar, mustard, salt, and black pepper into a small mixing bowl and whisk to combine. Then whisk in the olive oil. Taste and adjust seasoning. You can also make this by placing all of the ingredients in a small mason jar and shaking vigorously to combine. That way you also have a perfect way to store any extras.

MY EVERYTHING MARINADE

MAKES ABOUT 2 CUPS

8 to 10 garlic cloves, grated or pressed

1 large shallot, minced

½ cup fresh orange juice

⅓ cup fresh lime juice

¼ cup fish sauce or soy sauce

1 cup vegetable oil, such as sunflower or grapeseed

A handful fresh cilantro, chopped

This is hands-down my always and everything marinade for beef, pork, chicken, fish, or vegetables. It has hybrid Asian and Mexican influences, using heavy amounts of citrus for the acidity but then fish sauce (or soy sauce) for the salty umami component. For me, the addition of orange juice is the perfect balancing act here because the sweetness rounds things out. It also cuts through the fat in richer dishes, such as short ribs. You can play around with ingredients here and make your own version by adding other aromatics or punchy flavors such as ginger, basil, scallions, or sesame oil.

BLEND all of the ingredients in a food processor or blender to combine. If you prefer to have more texture, whisk them together in a mixing bowl.

How to Confit Any Vegetable

As far as techniques go, the simple method of confit for vegetables is my favorite one for preparation, preservation, and, of course, flavor. The thing I love about this method is that you can confit a batch of, say, tomatoes, garlic, onions, or even mushrooms and eggplant, and it not only preserves them for months longer but it also renders flavor and leaves you with an infused oil that can be incorporated into other dishes and sauces.

While you can use the oven to make confit, my preferred approach is to use the stovetop because I like to do this in a pot where I can control the amount of olive oil, to avoid excess. Also, you're able to keep an eye on the cooking so you can achieve the texture you desire—especially if you want the vegetable to hold some shape. When confit-ing vegetables, it is important to use a good-quality olive oil. It is also nice to play around with the addition of whole dried spices, such as peppercorns, fennel seeds, or cumin seeds. Lastly, you can really go wild with experimenting with combining different vegetables. Garlic and shallot go great with every vegetable, and combining eggplant, tomato, and garlic is a way to create something extra magical.

Fresh vegetable(s) of your choice, whole or sliced depending on how you want to use them

Herbs, both fresh and dried

Spices, both fresh and dried

Good-quality extra-virgin olive oil

CHOOSE a pot that will comfortably fit the amount of vegetables you want to confit but that is not so large that you're using too much olive oil. Place the vegetables into the pot, along with the herbs and spices of your choice. Cover with olive oil so the vegetables are fully submerged. Simmer over very low heat for 30 minutes to 1 hour, depending on the size and density of your vegetables and how tender you want them to be. You can then use them how you wish or transfer to an airtight jar and store in the fridge. When stored in the fridge, they will last for a couple of months.

NOTE: If using fresh herbs and spices, they are best used whole so you can remove them after cooking.

MY PERSONAL FAVORITES

While you can confit any vegetable using this method, these are some of my personal favorite things to confit.

Tomato + shallot + garlic + basil

Eggplant + cumin seed

Mushrooms + pearl onion + thyme

Leeks + fennel seed

Potatoes + rosemary + garlic

Acknowledgments

I believe one of the most important things about writing a cookbook and bringing it to life is to surround yourself with people, places, and things that inspire you and support you. And, with my move to Mexico several years ago, nothing has been more inspiring, supportive, and transformative as the community and the incredible surroundings here. Over the past few years, I am proud to say that I have found the most amazing community of friends, many of whom are creatives, chefs, photographers, design enthusiasts, etc., who have inspired me and awakened a new creative path that I never imagined before.

To start, I would like to thank David Alvarado who not only was our photographer for the book but is also my friend and colleague and was the first person I started working with to make this project happen. He encouraged me to bring this book to life and I am forever grateful for David's unwavering support and friendship.

All those conversations eventually lead me back to my amazing editor from my first book, *More with Less*. In the most serendipitous way, Juree got in touch with me after David and I already started to work on the beginnings of the book to see if I was interested in collaborating again. There was no hesitation that Juree's support and partnership through this process was the way to go, and once again I couldn't be prouder of what we have produced together—this time around with her top-notch design and marketing teams at Gibbs Smith.

And once the book production was underway, my good friends Liz (art director) and Aliza (creative production) jumped in to lend their creativity, as well as to cook and taste, and help pick out plates and backgrounds, but also to help with the less glamorous bits like dishes and grocery schlepping, all while enjoying many laughs and mezcals. There is no better experience than collaborating with your friends on something like this. Special shout out to Bella for jumping in and lending a (beautiful) hand (literally) during a few of our shoots. I feel so lucky to be surrounded by these inspiring women.

And to my Agustin, the best sous chef, taste tester, grill master. Your insatiable appetite for both food and life make each day an adventure, and your knowledge and love of Mexico and it's tacos has always impressed and excited me. You rouse my creativity and make me want to fill each day to the brim with fun, laughter, joy, and all the most delicious things. I love you, and our furry family (Coco, Luca, and Tita) so very much.

Lastly, I want to dedicate this book to my sweet angel Rhonda. Rhonda was my best friend and idol—the person I looked up to so much and who I aspired to be. She always treated each person she met with an extreme warmth and kindness, and everyone she touched instantly wanted to be her best friend. She was also the most supportive friend a girl could ask for. One of her last texts to me read: "Happy Sunday amiga bonita, James Beard is waiting for your work," along with a picture she took when she joined me at the James Beard awards for *More with Less*. Those are the kinds of friendships that make you shine and thrive, and I insist on living my life in that way and treating people in that way to honor the best friend I've ever known. This is for you, Rhonda. I did it (!) and so much is because of you.

INDEX

Metric Conversion Chart

Volume Measurements		Weight Measurements		Temperature Conversion	
U.S.	METRIC	U.S.	METRIC	FAHRENHEIT	CELSIUS
1 teaspoon	5 ml	1/2 ounce	15 g	250	120
1 tablespoon	15 ml	1 ounce	30 g	300	150
1/4 cup	60 ml	3 ounces	90 g	325	160
1/3 cup	75 ml	4 ounces	115 g	350	180
1/2 cup	125 ml	8 ounces	225 g	375	190
2/3 cup	150 ml	12 ounces	350 g	400	200
3/4 cup	175 ml	1 pound	450 g	425	220
1 cup	250 ml	2 1/4 pounds	1 kg	450	230

ABOUT THE AUTHOR

jodi moreno is a chef, culinary consultant, and food stylist. She is also the author of the James Beard–nominated cookbook, *More with Less: Whole Food Cooking Made Irresistibly Simple*. Her client list includes brands such Veuve Clicquot, Krug Champagne, Mastercard, One & Only Resorts, West Elm, KitchenAid, and more.

Her recipes and work have been featured by *Bon Appétit*, *Vogue*, *Saveur*, *Jamie Magazine*, *The Washington Post*, among others. Originally from New York City, Jodi eventually followed her tastes and her heart to Mexico City, where she now calls home. More recently, her love of dinner parties and insatiable appetite for travel has inspired her pop-up dinner parties that she shares all over the world.

First Edition
29 28 27 26 25   5 4 3 2 1

Text © 2025 Jodi Moreno
Photographs © 2025 David Alvarado

Additional photos by:
Jodi Moreno: 2, 10, 12, 30, 32, 48, 52, 54 upper left and right and middle, 62 bottom right,
72, 74 upper left and right and bottom, 82, 87, 124 upper right, 130, 142, 144, 193, and 195
Noel Higareda: author photo on page 207

Published by
Gibbs Smith
570 N Sportsplex Drive
Kaysville, Utah, 84037
1.800.835.4993 orders
www.gibbs-smith.com

Designed by The Sly Studio
Printed and bound in China

This product is made of FSC®-certified and other controlled material.

Library of Congress Control Number: 2024941754
ISBN: 978-1-4236-6738-4